Crack the C Programming In

101 Essential Questions & Answers for Job Seekers

By Sarful Hassan

Preface

Crack the C Programming Interview: 101 Essential Questions & Answers for Job Seekers was created to help candidates build confidence and technical competence when facing C programming interviews. Whether you are preparing for your first technical job or brushing up for an embedded systems role, this book provides structured, clear answers to the most important topics.

Who This Book Is For

- Students preparing for their first technical interviews

- Professionals seeking roles in software, embedded systems, or firmware development

- Self-learners wanting to strengthen their C programming fundamentals

- Anyone aiming to build a solid foundation in C for technical interviews

How This Book Is Organized

The book is divided into five logical sections:

1. **C Basics & Syntax (1–25):** Core concepts and structure of C programs.

2. **Functions, Arrays & Strings (26–50):** Modular programming and data structures.

3. **Pointers & Memory Management (51–75):** In-depth look at memory handling.

4. **Structures, Unions & Preprocessors (76–90):** Advanced C constructs.

5. **Advanced & Practical Scenarios (91–101):** Real-world applications and debugging.

Each question is designed to be self-contained, with beginner and experienced level answers, examples, and important tips.

What Was Left Out

This book focuses solely on C interview preparation. It does not cover:

- Full project-based tutorials
- GUI programming or complex OS-level C programming
- Detailed compiler design or system internals

Code Style (About the Code)

- Simple, readable C code
- Consistent indentation and naming conventions
- Portable and standard C (ANSI C / ISO C90 compliant wherever applicable)
- Focused on clarity rather than optimization tricks

Release Notes

This is the **First Edition (2025)**. Feedback from readers and interview candidates will be used to update and improve future editions.

Notes on the First Edition

While every effort has been made to ensure accuracy, minor errors may exist. We appreciate feedback and corrections from our readers to make this book even better.

MechatronicsLAB Online Learning

Visit **MechatronicsLAB** for more books, free resources, and online courses:

- Website: mechatronicslab.net
- Email: mechatronicslab.net@gmail.com

We are committed to helping you master technical skills and succeed in your career.

How to Contact Us

If you find errors, have suggestions, or want to collaborate, please reach out:

- Email: mechatronicslab.net@gmail.com

- Website: mechatronicslab.net

Acknowledgments for the First Edition

Thanks to the MechatronicsLAB team, early reviewers, students, and technical mentors whose feedback helped shape this book.

Copyright (MechatronicsLAB)

Disclaimer

Table of Contents

Section 1: C Basics & Syntax (1–25)

Interview Question 1: What Is C Language?

Why This Question Is Asked:

C is one of the most fundamental programming languages in computer science and embedded systems. Interviewers ask this to test your understanding of its purpose, strengths, and how it applies to system-level programming.

What the Interviewer Wants to Know:

- Do you understand what C language is used for?
- Can you explain its key features?
- Do you know why C is widely used in embedded systems?

How to Structure Your Answer:

1. Define what C language is
2. Mention its key features and advantages
3. Explain its relevance to embedded systems or systems programming

Sample Answer (Beginner):

"C is a general-purpose, high-level programming language developed in the 1970s. It's known for its simplicity, speed, and control over hardware. It's widely used to write programs for operating systems, compilers, and embedded systems because it allows low-level memory access and efficient execution."

Sample Answer (Experienced):

"C is a structured programming language that offers both low-level hardware access and high-level programming capabilities. It's commonly used in embedded systems development due to its portability, deterministic behavior, and minimal runtime overhead. C allows direct manipulation of memory through pointers, making it suitable for developing firmware, device drivers, and real-time applications."

Beginner Tip:

Focus on how C bridges the gap between machine language and modern programming. It's powerful because it's close to the hardware, but still readable.

Final Thought:

C is a foundational skill in embedded systems and systems programming. A good answer shows you understand its role and value, especially in performance-critical applications.

Interview Question 2: Who Developed the C Language?

Why This Question Is Asked:

Understanding the history of a programming language gives context to its design philosophy and relevance. Interviewers ask this question to see if you have a foundational awareness of C language origins.

What the Interviewer Wants to Know:

- Do you know the origin of the C language?
- Can you identify the key individual or organization involved?
- Are you aware of the historical context in which it was developed?

How to Structure Your Answer:

1. Name the developer of the C language
2. Mention when and where it was developed
3. Explain why it was developed and how it evolved

Sample Answer (Beginner):

"The C language was developed by Dennis Ritchie in the early 1970s at Bell Labs. It was created as an evolution of the B language to help build the UNIX operating system."

"C was developed by Dennis Ritchie between 1969 and 1973 at Bell Laboratories. It was designed to improve upon the B language and provide a structured yet low-level programming tool for systems programming. One of its main achievements was its role in the development of the UNIX operating system, which was later rewritten in C, showcasing its portability and efficiency."

Beginner Tip:

Remember the name Dennis Ritchie and Bell Labs—these are often key details interviewers expect.

Final Thought:

Knowing who created C and why helps you appreciate its role in modern computing history, especially in systems programming and operating system development.

Interview Question 3: What Are the Key Features of C?

Why This Question Is Asked:

Interviewers ask this to gauge your understanding of what makes C powerful and why it remains widely used despite being an older language.

What the Interviewer Wants to Know:

- Can you list the important features of the C language?
- Do you understand how these features benefit developers?
- Can you relate them to real-world programming scenarios?

How to Structure Your Answer:

1. List several core features of C
2. Explain each feature briefly
3. Optionally, relate features to embedded or systems programming

Sample Answer (Beginner):

"C is known for its simplicity, speed, and efficiency. It offers features like structured programming, low-level memory access using pointers, portability, and a rich set of built-in operators. It also supports modular programming through functions, making it easy to break programs into manageable parts."

Sample Answer (Experienced):

"The C language provides several key features:

- **Portability**: Programs written in C can be easily transferred between different machines.
- **Efficiency**: C generates fast-executing code and is ideal for performance-critical applications.
- **Low-level Access**: Direct memory manipulation is possible using pointers, useful for system-level programming.
- **Modularity**: Code can be organized into functions and files for better readability and reuse.
- **Rich Library Support**: Although basic, C's standard library supports essential operations.
- **Structured Language**: Encourages clean coding practices with conditionals, loops, and functions."

Beginner Tip:

Start by memorizing 3–4 important features and understand how they help build efficient programs.

Final Thought:

The strengths of C lie in its simplicity, power, and closeness to the hardware. These features make it a preferred choice for operating systems, embedded systems, and other system-level software.

Interview Question 4: What Is a Compiler?

Why This Question Is Asked:

Understanding the role of a compiler is fundamental for any programmer. Interviewers ask this question to test your grasp of the program translation process from high-level code to machine code.

What the Interviewer Wants to Know:

- Can you define what a compiler is?
- Do you understand its function in the software development process?
- Can you distinguish it from an interpreter?

How to Structure Your Answer:

1. Define what a compiler is
2. Explain its role in translating code
3. Mention how it differs from interpreters (if relevant)

Sample Answer (Beginner):

"A compiler is a software tool that translates high-level programming code into machine code so that a computer can execute it. It processes the entire program at once and generates an executable file."

Sample Answer (Experienced):

"A compiler is a program that converts source code written in a high-level language (like C or C++) into machine code, which is directly executable by the computer's CPU. It performs various tasks such as lexical analysis, syntax analysis, semantic analysis, optimization, and code generation. Unlike interpreters, compilers translate the entire code before execution, resulting in faster runtime performance."

Beginner Tip:

Remember: A compiler translates the *whole* code at once and generates an executable. This is different from interpreters that run code *line by line*.

Final Thought:

Compilers are essential for building efficient and optimized software. A good understanding of how they work can help you write better, more performant code.

Interview Question 5: How Is C Different from C++?

Why This Question Is Asked:

C and C++ are closely related, but they serve different programming needs. Interviewers ask this to evaluate your understanding of programming paradigms and language capabilities.

What the Interviewer Wants to Know:

- Do you understand the core differences between C and C++?
- Can you explain the conceptual shift from procedural to object-oriented programming?
- Are you aware of how these differences impact software design and development?

How to Structure Your Answer:

1. Start with a general comparison
2. Highlight key differences (syntax, paradigms, features)
3. Mention typical use cases for each language

Sample Answer (Beginner):
"C is a procedural programming language, while C++ is an extension of C that supports object-oriented programming. C++ allows classes and objects, making it easier to model real-world systems, while C focuses more on structured, function-based programming."

Sample Answer (Experienced):

"C is a procedural language primarily used for system-level programming and embedded systems. C++ builds on C by introducing object-oriented programming (OOP) features like classes, inheritance, and polymorphism, which support modular, reusable, and scalable code design. C++ also includes features such as function overloading, templates, exception handling, and the Standard Template Library (STL). While C provides fine-grained control over hardware, C++ adds abstraction and complexity management."

Beginner Tip:

Think of C as a building block language and C++ as an evolution that adds structure and abstraction.

Final Thought:

C is ideal for hardware-focused, resource-constrained projects. C++ is better suited for large-scale software development where abstraction and reusability are crucial.

Interview Question 6: What Is the Structure of a C Program?

Why This Question Is Asked:

Understanding the structure of a C program is essential for writing and debugging C code. This question tests your familiarity with how a typical C program is organized.

What the Interviewer Wants to Know:

- Do you understand the key components of a C program?
- Can you describe how a C program is typically written and executed?
- Are you able to explain the logical flow and function of each part?

How to Structure Your Answer:

1. List the main components of a C program
2. Briefly describe the purpose of each part
3. Optionally include a simple example or layout

Sample Answer (Beginner):

"A basic C program has the following structure:

1. **Preprocessor Directives** – like `#include <stdio.h>` for including standard libraries.
2. **Main Function** – the entry point of the program (`int main()`).
3. **Variable Declarations** – defining variables used in the program.
4. **Statements and Expressions** – the core logic or functionality.
5. **Return Statement** – returns a value to the operating system."

Sample Answer (Experienced):

"A C program generally consists of several structured sections:

- **Documentation Section**: Comments describing the program.
- **Link Section**: Includes header files (`#include`).
- **Definition Section**: Defines constants and macros (`#define`).
- **Global Declaration Section**: Declares global variables and functions.
- **Main Function Section**: `int main()` function where execution begins.
- **Subprogram Section**: User-defined functions used to modularize code."

Beginner Tip:
Focus on understanding the flow from top to bottom: headers → main → logic → return.

Final Thought:

A clear understanding of program structure helps you write organized, error-free code and enhances your debugging and collaboration skills.

Interview Question 7: How Do You Declare and Initialize Variables in C?

Why This Question Is Asked:

Variables are the foundation of programming logic. Interviewers ask this to evaluate your understanding of data types, memory allocation, and proper coding syntax in C.

What the Interviewer Wants to Know:

- Do you know how to declare variables in C?
- Can you correctly initialize variables during or after declaration?
- Do you understand basic data types and usage?

How to Structure Your Answer:

1. Explain variable declaration syntax
2. Describe initialization during declaration and post-declaration
3. Provide examples of common data types (int, float, char, etc.)

Sample Answer (Beginner):

"In C, you declare a variable by specifying its data type followed by its name. For example, `int age;` declares an integer variable. You can also initialize it at the time of declaration like `int age = 25;`."

Sample Answer (Experienced):

"Variable declaration in C follows the format: `<data_type> <variable_name>;`. You can also combine declaration and initialization, e.g., `float temperature = 36.5;`. C supports several data types such as `int`, `float`, `char`, and `double`. You can declare multiple variables in one line: `int a = 5, b = 10;`. Initialization helps avoid undefined behavior due to garbage values."

Beginner Tip:

Always initialize variables before using them to prevent bugs.

Final Thought:

Proper declaration and initialization of variables ensure predictable program behavior and reduce memory-related errors.

Interview Question 8: What Are Data Types in C?

Why This Question Is Asked:

Understanding data types is essential for memory management and type safety. Interviewers use this question to assess your foundational knowledge of how C handles different kinds of data.

What the Interviewer Wants to Know:

- Can you define what data types are?
- Do you know the main categories of data types in C?
- Can you explain how data types affect memory usage and operations?

How to Structure Your Answer:

1. Define what data types are in C
2. List primary categories (basic, derived, user-defined, void)
3. Give examples and describe their typical use cases

Sample Answer (Beginner):

"Data types in C define the type of data a variable can store. Common data types include `int` for integers, `float` for decimal numbers, and `char` for characters. Each data type uses different amounts of memory and has a specific range of values."

Sample Answer (Experienced):

"C has several categories of data types:

- **Basic Types**: int, char, float, double.
- **Derived Types**: arrays, pointers, functions.
- **Enumeration Types**: enum for defining named integer constants.
- **User-Defined Types**: struct, union, and typedef.
- **Void Type**: represents no value, commonly used in functions that return nothing. Understanding the size, range, and behavior of each type is critical for efficient memory management and safe programming."

Beginner Tip:

Start with learning basic data types (int, char, float) and gradually explore advanced types as you practice more coding.

Final Thought:

Choosing the right data type is crucial for program efficiency and clarity. A strong grasp of data types helps prevent bugs and makes your code more robust.

Interview Question 9: What Are Constants in C?

Why This Question Is Asked:

Constants are essential for maintaining fixed values throughout a program. Interviewers ask this to check if you understand how to define unchangeable values and use them efficiently in C.

What the Interviewer Wants to Know:

- Can you define what a constant is?
- Do you know how to declare constants?
- Are you familiar with different types of constants in C?

How to Structure Your Answer:

1. Define constants in C
2. Mention ways to declare constants (`const`, `#define`)
3. Explain types of constants (integer, float, character, string)

Sample Answer (Beginner):

"Constants in C are fixed values that do not change during program execution. You can define them using the `const` keyword like `const int max = 100;` or with `#define` preprocessor directives like `#define MAX 100`."

Sample Answer (Experienced):

"In C, constants are immutable values defined using either the `const` keyword or the `#define` macro. `const` defines a typed constant, while `#define` replaces text before compilation. Constants can be of various types:

- **Integer constants**: `const int a = 10;`
- **Floating-point constants**: `const float pi = 3.14;`
- **Character constants**: `const char ch = 'A';`
- **String constants**: string literals like `"Hello"`. Using constants improves code readability, maintainability, and safety."

Beginner Tip:

Prefer `const` over `#define` for typed constants in modern C programming.

Final Thought:

Constants help make programs more understandable and less error-prone. Knowing how to use them properly is a mark of good coding practice.

Interview Question 10: What Are Keywords? Name 5.

Why This Question Is Asked:

Keywords are the backbone of any programming language. Interviewers use this question to test your understanding of reserved words in C and their roles in program structure.

What the Interviewer Wants to Know:

- Do you understand what keywords are?
- Can you identify them and explain their purpose?
- Are you aware that keywords cannot be used as identifiers?

How to Structure Your Answer:

1. Define what keywords are in C
2. Explain their role and restrictions
3. List and describe 5 commonly used keywords

Sample Answer (Beginner):

"Keywords in C are reserved words that have special meanings defined by the language. They cannot be used as variable names or identifiers. Examples include int, return, if, else, and while."

Sample Answer (Experienced):

"Keywords are predefined, reserved identifiers in the C language used to perform specific operations or define program structure. They form the syntax and grammar of C and cannot be redefined or used as variable names. Five common C keywords are:

- int: used to declare integer variables.
- return: exits from a function and optionally returns a value.
- if: starts a conditional control statement.
- while: starts a loop that continues while a condition is true.
- void: indicates no return type for functions."

Beginner Tip:

Memorize the most commonly used keywords and understand their basic function.

Final Thought:

A solid understanding of keywords is vital for writing valid and functional C programs. They form the foundation of all syntax and logic structures.

Interview Question 11: What Is the Difference Between printf() and scanf()?

Why This Question Is Asked:

These two functions are essential in C for basic input and output operations. Interviewers ask this to evaluate your understanding of how data is read and displayed in a C program.

What the Interviewer Wants to Know:

- Do you know the purpose of `printf()` and `scanf()`?
- Can you explain how each function is used?
- Are you aware of the syntax and format specifiers involved?

How to Structure Your Answer:

1. Define both `printf()` and `scanf()` functions
2. Explain their roles in a program
3. Highlight the main differences with examples

Sample Answer (Beginner):

"`printf()` is used to display output to the screen, while `scanf()` is used to take input from the user. For example, `printf("Enter a number:");` displays a message, and `scanf("%d", &num);` reads an integer value into the variable num."

Sample Answer (Experienced):

"The printf() function outputs data to the standard output (usually the screen), and uses format specifiers like %d for integers or %s for strings. scanf() reads formatted input from the standard input (keyboard), using similar format specifiers but requires variable addresses (e.g., &var) to store the input values. The key difference lies in direction—printf() sends data out, while scanf() receives data in."

Beginner Tip:

Always use the address-of (&) operator with scanf() to store input values correctly.

Final Thought:

Both printf() and scanf() are foundational for C programming. Mastering them is essential for user interaction in console-based applications.

Interview Question 12: What Are Format Specifiers?

Why This Question Is Asked:

Format specifiers are essential for data input/output operations in C. Interviewers ask this question to test your familiarity with data types and how to display or accept them using printf() and scanf().

What the Interviewer Wants to Know:

- Do you understand what format specifiers are?
- Can you identify the common ones and their usage?
- Can you apply them correctly in real code examples?

How to Structure Your Answer:

1. Define what format specifiers are
2. Explain their use in printf() and scanf()
3. List common specifiers with examples

Sample Answer (Beginner):

"Format specifiers are placeholders used in `printf()` and `scanf()` to indicate the type of data being printed or read. For example, %d is used for integers, %f for floating-point numbers, and %c for characters."

Sample Answer (Experienced):

"Format specifiers in C define the type of data to be input or output. They are used within `printf()` and `scanf()` to ensure correct interpretation of variables. Common specifiers include:

- %d or %i – for integers
- %f – for float
- %lf – for double
- %c – for characters
- %s – for strings Each specifier corresponds to a specific data type and helps the compiler correctly handle memory and type conversions."

Beginner Tip:

Make sure the data type of the variable matches the format specifier to avoid unexpected behavior.

Final Thought:

Format specifiers are a vital part of C I/O functions. Understanding them ensures that user input and program output are handled accurately and safely.

Interview Question 13: What Is a Header File?

Why This Question Is Asked:

Header files are essential for modular and reusable code in C. Interviewers ask this question to test your understanding of how C programs are structured and compiled.

What the Interviewer Wants to Know:

- Do you know what header files are used for?
- Can you explain their role in organizing and reusing code?
- Are you familiar with standard vs. user-defined header files?

How to Structure Your Answer:

1. Define what a header file is
2. Explain its purpose and contents
3. Mention standard and user-defined header files with examples

Sample Answer (Beginner):

"A header file in C contains function declarations, macros, and sometimes type definitions. It allows code to be reused across multiple files. For example, `#include <stdio.h>` includes standard input-output functions."

Sample Answer (Experienced):

"Header files in C contain declarations for functions, constants, macros, and data types, which are shared across multiple source files. Standard header files like `<stdio.h>` or `<math.h>` include library functions, while user-defined header files (e.g., `myfunctions.h`) help in modularizing large projects. They are included using the `#include` directive during preprocessing. This enables better code organization and reuse."

Beginner Tip:

Always use angle brackets (`<>`) for standard headers and double quotes (`""`) for user-defined ones.

Final Thought:

Header files simplify code maintenance and encourage reusable, modular programming. Knowing how to use them properly is a must for every C programmer.

Interview Question 14: What Is the Purpose of main() Function?

Why This Question Is Asked:

The main() function is the entry point of any C program. Interviewers ask this to confirm you understand how program execution begins and the significance of main().

What the Interviewer Wants to Know:

- Do you understand the role of main() in a C program?
- Can you describe its syntax and behavior?
- Do you know about its return value and arguments?

How to Structure Your Answer:

1. Define the main() function and its role
2. Describe standard syntax and return type
3. Explain how arguments (argc, argv) may be used

Sample Answer (Beginner):

"The main() function is the starting point of a C program. When a program runs, execution begins with the code inside main(). It typically returns an integer to indicate success or failure."

Sample Answer (Experienced):

"In C, the main() function serves as the entry point of the program. It can be defined as int main() or int main(int argc, char *argv[]). The int return type is used to return an exit status to the operating system, with 0 typically meaning successful execution. argc counts the number of command-line arguments, and argv holds them as strings. This setup enables dynamic input from the command line."

Beginner Tip:

Always include a return statement like `return 0;` to indicate successful program termination.

Final Thought:

Understanding `main()` is critical because it's the foundation of every C program. It's where execution starts and typically where it ends.

Interview Question 15: What Are the Arithmetic Operators in C?

Why This Question Is Asked:

Arithmetic operators are fundamental in programming for performing calculations. Interviewers ask this question to assess your knowledge of basic operators and how they are used in expressions.

What the Interviewer Wants to Know:
- Do you know the different arithmetic operators in C?
- Can you use them correctly in expressions?
- Are you familiar with how they work with different data types?

How to Structure Your Answer:
1. Define what arithmetic operators are
2. List and explain each operator
3. Give simple examples using each one

Sample Answer (Beginner):
"Arithmetic operators in C are used to perform basic mathematical operations. The five main arithmetic operators are:

- `+` for addition
- `-` for subtraction
- `*` for multiplication
- `/` for division
- `%` for modulus (remainder) For example: `int sum = a + b;`"

Sample Answer (Experienced):

"C provides five primary arithmetic operators:

- + (Addition): Adds two operands.
- - (Subtraction): Subtracts the second operand from the first.
- * (Multiplication): Multiplies two operands.
- / (Division): Divides the numerator by the denominator (integer division if both operands are integers).
- % (Modulus): Returns the remainder of integer division. Each operator follows standard precedence rules and can be combined in expressions. Typecasting may be required when mixing data types."

Beginner Tip:

Be careful when using / and %—they work only with integers unless typecasting is applied.

Final Thought:

Mastering arithmetic operators is crucial for any C programmer. They are the building blocks for all kinds of numeric logic and calculations.

Interview Question 16: What Is Typecasting?

Why This Question Is Asked:

Typecasting is essential when working with mixed data types. Interviewers ask this to evaluate your understanding of how data types can be converted to ensure accurate computations and memory management.

What the Interviewer Wants to Know:

- Can you define typecasting in C?
- Do you know the difference between implicit and explicit typecasting?
- Can you explain when and why typecasting is necessary?

How to Structure Your Answer:

1. Define typecasting
2. Explain its types (implicit and explicit)
3. Provide examples where typecasting is used

Sample Answer (Beginner):

"Typecasting means converting one data type into another. For example, converting a `float` to an `int`. It helps in operations where both operands must be of the same type."

Sample Answer (Experienced):

"Typecasting in C is the process of converting a variable from one data type to another. It can be:

- **Implicit Typecasting**: Automatically done by the compiler when converting from a smaller to a larger data type (e.g., `int` to `float`).
- **Explicit Typecasting**: Manually done by the programmer using cast operators, like `(int)3.14` which results in 3. Typecasting is especially important in expressions involving different data types to avoid unexpected results or loss of precision."

Beginner Tip:

Always use explicit typecasting when precision or data loss could be an issue.

Final Thought:

Understanding typecasting ensures better control over program behavior, particularly when handling arithmetic operations and function return types.

Interview Question 17: What Is Precedence and Associativity?

Why This Question Is Asked:

Operator precedence and associativity determine the order in which expressions are evaluated. Interviewers ask this to assess your understanding of expression evaluation and how it affects program logic.

What the Interviewer Wants to Know:

- Can you define precedence and associativity?
- Do you know how they influence expression evaluation?
- Can you provide examples to illustrate the concepts?

How to Structure Your Answer:

1. Define precedence and associativity separately
2. Explain how they affect multi-operator expressions
3. Provide examples showing correct and incorrect assumptions

Sample Answer (Beginner):

"Precedence determines which operator is evaluated first when there are multiple operators in an expression. Associativity tells us the direction in which operators of the same precedence are evaluated—either left to right or right to left."

Sample Answer (Experienced):

"In C, **precedence** refers to the priority of operators in expressions. For example, multiplication has higher precedence than addition, so 2 + 3 * 4 is evaluated as 2 + (3 * 4) = 14. **Associativity** defines the direction (left-to-right or right-to-left) in which operators of the same precedence level are evaluated. Most operators, like + and -, are left-associative, while assignment operators (=) are right-associative. These rules ensure consistent and predictable evaluation of expressions."

Beginner Tip:

Use parentheses to make the order of operations clear and avoid logical errors.

Final Thought:

Knowing precedence and associativity is crucial for writing correct and efficient expressions, especially in complex calculations.

Interview Question 18: What Is an Expression?

Why This Question Is Asked:

Expressions are at the core of programming logic. Interviewers ask this to test your understanding of how values are computed and manipulated in C.

What the Interviewer Wants to Know:

- Can you define what an expression is in C?
- Do you understand how expressions are evaluated?
- Can you provide examples of different types of expressions?

How to Structure Your Answer:

1. Define an expression in C
2. Describe different types of expressions (arithmetic, logical, relational, etc.)
3. Give examples to illustrate

Sample Answer (Beginner):

"An expression in C is a combination of variables, constants, and operators that produces a value. For example, a + b is an arithmetic expression that adds two values."

"In C, an expression is any valid combination of literals, variables, operators, and function calls that evaluates to a single value. Types of expressions include:

- **Arithmetic Expressions**: x + y * 2
- **Relational Expressions**: a > b
- **Logical Expressions**: x && y
- **Assignment Expressions**: a = b + 1 Each expression is evaluated based on operator precedence and associativity rules."

Beginner Tip:

Every expression must return a value, and its type depends on the types of its components.

Final Thought:

Understanding expressions is fundamental to controlling program logic, computations, and decision-making in C.

Interview Question 19: How Do You Take User Input in C?

Why This Question Is Asked:

User input is essential for interactive programs. This question tests your understanding of standard input functions and safe input handling in C.

What the Interviewer Wants to Know:

- Do you know how to use scanf() or related functions?
- Can you correctly match format specifiers with variable types?
- Are you aware of common pitfalls in user input handling?

How to Structure Your Answer:

1. Explain the use of input functions like `scanf()`
2. Mention format specifiers and variable addresses
3. Provide an example and discuss input validation if needed

Sample Answer (Beginner):

"To take user input in C, we use the `scanf()` function. For example, `scanf("%d", &number);` takes an integer input and stores it in the variable number. The & symbol is used to provide the address of the variable."

Sample Answer (Experienced):

"C uses standard input functions like `scanf()` to take user input. `scanf()` requires format specifiers to match the type of the input variable (e.g., %d for integers, %f for floats). You must use the address-of operator (&) to store the input value in the variable. Example:

```
int age;
printf("Enter your age: ");
scanf("%d", &age);
```

For strings, `scanf("%s", str);` is used, but it doesn't handle spaces. Safer alternatives like `fgets()` can be used for reading full lines."

Beginner Tip:

Always verify that the format specifier matches the variable type, and be careful with spaces in string input.

Final Thought:

Accurate input handling ensures your program behaves as expected and prevents common bugs or vulnerabilities.

Interview Question 20: What Are Control Statements?

Why This Question Is Asked:

Control statements allow decision-making and repetition in programs. Interviewers ask this to evaluate your understanding of how program flow is managed in C.

What the Interviewer Wants to Know:

- Can you define control statements in C?
- Do you know the types of control statements?
- Can you explain their role in decision-making and loops?

How to Structure Your Answer:

1. Define what control statements are
2. List and briefly describe the main types
3. Provide examples of each type

Sample Answer (Beginner):

"Control statements in C are used to control the flow of execution of the program. The main types are:

- **Conditional Statements**: `if, if-else, switch`
- **Looping Statements**: `for, while, do-while`
- **Jump Statements**: `break, continue, goto, return`"

Sample Answer (Experienced):

"Control statements in C determine the direction in which the program flows based on conditions and repetitions. They are categorized into:

1. **Decision-Making Statements**:
   a. `if, if-else, nested if, switch`
2. **Looping Statements**:
   a. `for, while, do-while` — used for repeating a block of

code

3. **Jump Statements**:
    a. break (exits a loop), continue (skips to the next iteration), goto (jumps to a labeled statement), return (exits from a function) These statements provide structure, flexibility, and logic to programs."

Beginner Tip:

Start with understanding if-else and for loops—these are the most commonly used control statements.

Final Thought:

Mastering control statements is crucial for writing efficient and logical programs. They allow your code to adapt to different situations and perform repetitive tasks.

Interview Question 21: How Do You Write an if-else Block in C?

Why This Question Is Asked:

The if-else statement is the foundation of decision-making in C. Interviewers ask this question to see if you understand conditional execution and can apply it correctly.

What the Interviewer Wants to Know:

- Can you write the correct syntax for an if-else block?
- Do you understand how conditions control program flow?
- Can you apply if, else if, and else constructs effectively?

How to Structure Your Answer:

1. Describe what an if-else block is
2. Explain the syntax and flow
3. Provide a code example

Sample Answer (Beginner):

"An `if-else` block is used to execute different code based on whether a condition is true or false. Here is an example:

```
int num = 10;
if (num > 0) {
    printf("Positive number\n");
} else {
    printf("Non-positive number\n");
}
```

If the condition in `if` is true, the code inside it runs. Otherwise, the `else` block runs."

Sample Answer (Experienced):

"The `if-else` structure enables branching logic in C. It evaluates a condition and executes a corresponding block of code. You can also chain multiple conditions using `else if`. Example:

```
int score = 85;
if (score >= 90) {
    printf("Grade A\n");
} else if (score >= 75) {
    printf("Grade B\n");
} else {
    printf("Grade C or below\n");
}
```

This structure helps in decision-making where multiple outcomes are possible."

Beginner Tip:

Always use curly braces {} even for single-line statements to avoid bugs.

Final Thought:

`if-else` blocks are essential for dynamic program behavior. Understanding their syntax and logic flow is key to writing responsive C programs.

Interview Question 22: What Is the Syntax of switch-case?

Why This Question Is Asked:

The switch-case statement is useful for handling multiple fixed-value conditions. Interviewers ask this to evaluate your understanding of alternative decision-making structures in C.

What the Interviewer Wants to Know:

- Do you understand how switch-case works?
- Can you write its correct syntax?
- Do you know when to use it instead of if-else?

How to Structure Your Answer:

1. Explain what switch-case is
2. Describe its syntax and how it functions
3. Provide an example for clarity

Sample Answer (Beginner):

"The switch-case statement checks the value of a variable against multiple cases. If a match is found, that case block is executed. Example:

```c
int day = 3;
switch (day) {
    case 1:
        printf("Monday\n");
        break;
    case 2:
        printf("Tuesday\n");
        break;
    case 3:
        printf("Wednesday\n");
        break;
    default:
        printf("Invalid day\n");
}
```

The break statement exits the switch block after a case is executed."

Sample Answer (Experienced):

"The switch-case construct is an efficient alternative to multiple if-else conditions when dealing with discrete constant values. Its syntax is:

```
switch (expression) {
    case constant1:
        // statements
        break;
    case constant2:
        // statements
        break;
    ...
    default:
        // default statements
}
```

Each case matches the expression value. The default block is optional and runs if no case matches. Always use break to avoid fall-through, unless intentional."

Beginner Tip:

Forget to use break can cause unexpected fall-through behavior. Use it carefully.

Final Thought:

The switch-case structure simplifies decision-making with constant values, making code cleaner and more readable than long if-else chains.

Interview Question 23: What Are Loops in C?

Why This Question Is Asked:

Loops are fundamental for executing repetitive tasks efficiently. Interviewers ask this to assess your understanding of iterative control structures in C.

What the Interviewer Wants to Know:

- Can you define what loops are?
- Do you know the different types of loops in C?
- Can you apply them correctly with syntax and use cases?

How to Structure Your Answer:

1. Define loops and their purpose
2. List and describe each type (for, while, do-while)
3. Provide simple code examples

Sample Answer (Beginner):

"Loops in C are used to execute a block of code repeatedly while a condition is true. The main types of loops are:

- for loop: used when the number of iterations is known.
- while loop: used when the condition is checked before the loop.
- do-while loop: checks the condition after executing the loop body."

Sample Answer (Experienced):

"Loops allow repeated execution of a block of code based on a condition. C supports three primary loops:
- **for loop**: Ideal for fixed iteration counts.

```c
for (int i = 0; i < 5; i++) {
    printf("%d\n", i);
}
```

while loop: Executes as long as the condition is true.

```c
int i = 0;
while (i < 5) {
    printf("%d\n", i);
    i++;
}
```

- **do-while loop**: Similar to while, but guarantees one execution.

```c
int i = 0;
do {
    printf("%d\n", i);
    i++;
} while (i < 5);
```

Each loop has different use cases based on when the condition needs to be checked."

Beginner Tip:

Choose your loop based on when and how often you want to check the condition.

Final Thought:

Loops are essential for automation in programs. Mastering them helps in handling tasks like iteration, processing data, and algorithm implementation.

Interview Question 24: What Is the Difference Between while and do-while Loops?

Why This Question Is Asked:

Understanding the subtle difference between while and do-while loops is key to controlling loop execution accurately. Interviewers ask this to test your grasp of loop behavior and condition checking in C.

What the Interviewer Wants to Know:

- Do you understand how these loops differ in condition checking?
- Can you explain when to use each loop type?
- Are you aware of potential logic issues when choosing the wrong loop?

How to Structure Your Answer:

1. Explain the purpose of both loops
2. Highlight the key difference in condition checking
3. Show examples and use cases

Sample Answer (Beginner):

"The main difference is that a `while` loop checks the condition before the loop body runs, while a `do-while` loop checks the condition after running the body. This means `do-while` always runs at least once."

Sample Answer (Experienced):

"In C, both `while` and `do-while` are entry-controlled and exit-controlled loops respectively:

- **`while` loop**: Evaluates the condition first. If it's false initially, the loop body may not execute at all.

```
int i = 0;
while (i > 0) {
    printf("This won't print\n");
    i++;
}
```

- **`do-while` loop**: Executes the loop body once before evaluating the condition.

```
int i = 0;
do {
    printf("This prints at least once\n");
```

```
    i++;
} while (i > 0);
```

Use do-while when you want the code to execute at least once regardless of the condition."

Beginner Tip:

If you're not sure whether the condition will be true initially, and you still want the loop to run once, go with do-while.

Final Thought:

Choosing between while and do-while impacts how and when your code runs. Knowing their differences ensures correct logic flow.

Interview Question 25: What Is a Comment in C?

Why This Question Is Asked:

Comments are vital for code readability and maintenance. Interviewers ask this question to confirm your understanding of how to document code properly in C.

What the Interviewer Wants to Know:

- Can you define what a comment is?
- Do you know the syntax for writing comments in C?
- Do you understand the role comments play in code maintenance?

How to Structure Your Answer:

1. Define comments and their purpose
2. Describe the types of comments in C
3. Provide examples and best practices

Sample Answer (Beginner):

"Comments in C are notes written in the code to explain what the code does. They are ignored by the compiler and don't affect program execution. There are two types: single-line (//) and multi-line (/* */) comments."

Sample Answer (Experienced):

"In C, comments are non-executable lines that improve code readability and help with documentation. They are used to explain logic, clarify code sections, or temporarily disable parts of code during debugging. Types include:

- **Single-line comments**: Use // (e.g., `// This is a comment`)
- **Multi-line comments**: Use /* ... */ (e.g., `/* This is a multi-line comment */`) Good commenting improves collaboration and eases future maintenance."

Beginner Tip:

Use comments to explain 'why' something is done, not just 'what' is being done.

Final Thought:

Well-placed comments make code easier to understand and maintain, especially in team projects or large codebases.

Section 2: Functions, Arrays & Strings (26–50)

Interview Question 26: What Is a Function?

Why This Question Is Asked:

Functions are essential for code reuse and modularity. Interviewers ask this to check your understanding of how to structure and organize C programs effectively.

What the Interviewer Wants to Know:

- Can you define what a function is in C?
- Do you know the components of a function?
- Can you explain the advantages of using functions?

How to Structure Your Answer:

1. Define a function
2. Describe the syntax and components (name, return type, parameters, body)
3. Explain the benefits of using functions and give an example

Sample Answer (Beginner):
"A function in C is a block of code that performs a specific task. It has a name and can be called multiple times from other parts of the program. For example:
```
int add(int a, int b) {
    return a + b;
}
```
This function returns the sum of two integers."

Sample Answer (Experienced):

"In C, a function is a reusable and modular code block that performs a specific operation. It includes:

- **Return type**: Data type of the value the function returns (e.g., int, void)
- **Function name**: Identifier used to call the function
- **Parameters**: Inputs passed to the function
- **Function body**: Contains statements to execute Functions promote code reuse, readability, and easier debugging. Example:

```
float multiply(float x, float y) {
    return x * y;
}
```

This allows structured programming by breaking the code into smaller, manageable parts."

Beginner Tip:

Always declare functions before calling them, or place the definition above the main() function.

Final Thought:

Functions are fundamental building blocks in C programming. They improve code organization, support modularity, and make large programs easier to manage.

Interview Question 27: How Do You Define and Call a Function?

Why This Question Is Asked:

Functions are core to structured programming. Interviewers ask this to verify your understanding of defining reusable logic and invoking it correctly within a program.

What the Interviewer Wants to Know:

- Do you know how to write function definitions?
- Can you correctly call a function with appropriate arguments?
- Do you understand how return values work?

How to Structure Your Answer:

1. Describe how to define a function (return type, name, parameters, body)
2. Explain how to call a function
3. Provide a working example

Sample Answer (Beginner):

"To define a function, you write the return type, name, and parameters. For example:

```
int add(int a, int b) {
    return a + b;
}
```

To call this function, you write:

```
int result = add(3, 4);
```

This calls the function with 3 and 4 as arguments and stores the result."

Sample Answer (Experienced):

"A function in C is defined using the syntax:

```
<return_type> function_name(parameter_list) {
    // function body
    return value;
}
```

To call a function, use its name followed by parentheses containing arguments:

```
int result = add(5, 7);
```

You can define the function above the main() function or declare a prototype and define it later. For example:

```
// Function prototype
```

```
double square(double x);

// Function definition
double square(double x) {
    return x * x;
}

// Function call in main()
double result = square(3.5);
```

This structure improves code clarity and modularity."

Beginner Tip:

Make sure the function is declared or defined before it's called.

Final Thought:

Understanding function definition and invocation is crucial for modular, readable, and maintainable C programs.

Interview Question 28: What Are Function Arguments and Return Values?

Why This Question Is Asked:

Functions rely on arguments and return values to exchange data. Interviewers ask this to assess your understanding of how data flows into and out of functions in C.

What the Interviewer Wants to Know:

- Do you understand how to pass data to a function?
- Can you explain how a function returns a value?
- Are you familiar with the syntax and purpose of both?

How to Structure Your Answer:

1. Define what arguments and return values are
2. Describe how they are used in functions
3. Provide examples to show both

Sample Answer (Beginner):

"Function arguments are values you pass to a function so it can use them. A return value is what the function gives back after it finishes running. For example:

```
int add(int a, int b) { // a and b are arguments
    return a + b;        // returns the sum
}
```

You call it with values: `int result = add(3, 4);`"

Sample Answer (Experienced):

"In C, function **arguments** are the variables listed in a function's definition and receive values (known as **parameters**) from the function call. The **return value** is the result the function sends back to the caller using the `return` keyword. For example:

```
float multiply(float x, float y) {
    return x * y;
}
```

Here, x and y are arguments, and the function returns a `float` result. If no value is returned, the function uses the `void` return type."

Beginner Tip:

Match the number and type of arguments in the function definition and call to avoid errors.

Final Thought:

Understanding function arguments and return values is vital for breaking code into manageable, reusable blocks that communicate effectively.

Interview Question 29: What Is Recursion?

Why This Question Is Asked:

Recursion is a powerful technique for solving problems by dividing them into smaller subproblems. Interviewers ask this to test your understanding of advanced control flow and function usage.

What the Interviewer Wants to Know:

- Can you define recursion and recognize its structure?
- Do you understand the need for a base condition?
- Can you apply recursion to real problems like factorial, Fibonacci, etc.?

How to Structure Your Answer:

1. Define recursion
2. Explain how it works with an example
3. Highlight the importance of base cases and termination

Sample Answer (Beginner):

"Recursion is when a function calls itself to solve a smaller part of the problem. It continues to call itself until a base condition is met."

Sample Answer (Experienced):

"Recursion is a technique where a function solves a problem by calling itself with a smaller input. Each recursive call reduces the problem size, and a **base condition** ensures termination. For example:

```
int factorial(int n) {
    if (n == 0) return 1;              // base case
    else return n * factorial(n - 1);  // recursive
call
}
```

This function calculates the factorial of a number. Recursive solutions are elegant but should be used carefully to avoid stack overflow."

Beginner Tip:

Always write a base condition; otherwise, the function will call itself endlessly and crash the program.

Final Thought:

Recursion simplifies complex problems like tree traversal, backtracking, and divide-and-conquer algorithms. Mastery of recursion is a sign of strong problem-solving skills.

Interview Question 30: What Are Arrays?

Why This Question Is Asked:

Arrays are fundamental data structures in C. Interviewers ask this to assess your understanding of how to store and manage collections of data.

What the Interviewer Wants to Know:

- Can you define what an array is?
- Do you understand how to declare, access, and modify arrays?
- Are you aware of the benefits and limitations of using arrays?

How to Structure Your Answer:

1. Define what an array is in C
2. Explain how to declare and use it
3. Provide examples of common operations

Sample Answer (Beginner):

"An array is a collection of elements of the same type stored in contiguous memory locations. You can access each element using an index. Example:

```
int numbers[5] = {1, 2, 3, 4, 5};
printf("%d", numbers[0]); // prints 1
```

The first element has index 0, and the last element has index `size - 1`."

Sample Answer (Experienced):

"Arrays in C are fixed-size data structures that hold multiple elements of the same data type. They are useful for batch processing and indexed access. Syntax:

```
int arr[10]; // declares an integer array of size 10
arr[0] = 5;   // sets the first element
```

You can iterate through arrays using loops. However, arrays in C do not perform bounds checking, so care must be taken to avoid accessing out-of-range indices."

Beginner Tip:

Array indices start from 0, not 1. Accessing beyond the array size causes undefined behavior.

Final Thought:

Arrays are essential for storing lists of values efficiently. Mastery of arrays leads to better understanding of pointers, memory handling, and more complex data structures.

Interview Question 31: How Do You Declare and Initialize Arrays?

Why This Question Is Asked:

Knowing how to declare and initialize arrays correctly is crucial for managing structured data. Interviewers ask this to test your grasp of syntax and initialization rules in C.

What the Interviewer Wants to Know:

- Can you declare arrays with and without initialization?
- Do you understand how array sizes and indexes work?
- Can you demonstrate both static and dynamic initialization?

How to Structure Your Answer:

1. Explain the syntax for array declaration
2. Describe different initialization methods
3. Provide examples

Sample Answer (Beginner):

"To declare an array in C, specify the data type, array name, and size. Example:

```
int numbers[5];
```

To initialize it at the time of declaration:

```
int numbers[5] = {1, 2, 3, 4, 5};
```

You can also let the compiler count the elements:

```
int numbers[] = {1, 2, 3};
```

"

Sample Answer (Experienced):

"Arrays can be declared and initialized in several ways:

- **Static Initialization**:

```
char vowels[5] = {'a', 'e', 'i', 'o', 'u'};
```

- **Partial Initialization** (remaining elements set to 0):

```
int marks[5] = {10, 20}; // others default to 0
```

- **Compiler-determined size**:

```
float prices[] = {9.99, 14.99, 4.99};
```

These methods allow flexibility in how arrays are used and allocated."

Beginner Tip:

If you initialize an array at the time of declaration, you can omit the size.

Final Thought:

Mastering array declaration and initialization is fundamental to effective memory management and data organization in C.

Interview Question 32: What Is a Multi-Dimensional Array?

Why This Question Is Asked:

Multi-dimensional arrays are used for handling matrices or tabular data. Interviewers ask this to assess your knowledge of more complex data structures in C.

What the Interviewer Wants to Know:

- Can you define what a multi-dimensional array is?
- Do you understand how to declare, access, and initialize one?
- Can you provide examples and describe use cases?

How to Structure Your Answer:

1. Define multi-dimensional arrays
2. Describe declaration and initialization
3. Give examples and explain usage

Sample Answer (Beginner):

"A multi-dimensional array is an array of arrays. The most common is the 2D array, like a table with rows and columns. Example:

```
int matrix[2][3] = {
    {1, 2, 3},
    {4, 5, 6}
};
```

You access elements with two indices: `matrix[0][1]` is 2."

Sample Answer (Experienced):

"In C, multi-dimensional arrays are used to represent data in a grid-like structure. The syntax for declaring a 2D array is:

```
type arrayName[row][column];
```

For example:

```
float grades[3][4]; // 3 rows, 4 columns
```

You can initialize it with nested braces:

```
int grid[2][2] = {{1, 2}, {3, 4}};
```

Access is done using `array[i][j]`. This is especially useful in matrix operations, image processing, or board game simulations."

Beginner Tip:

Use nested loops to access or manipulate elements of a multi-dimensional array.

Final Thought:

Multi-dimensional arrays allow structured representation of complex data. Mastery of these is key for applications involving matrices or multi-layered information.

Interview Question 33: How Do You Pass Arrays to Functions?

Why This Question Is Asked:

Passing arrays to functions is essential for modular programming. Interviewers ask this to test your understanding of function parameters and memory handling in C.

What the Interviewer Wants to Know:

- Can you correctly pass arrays to functions?
- Do you understand how array decay works (arrays as pointers)?
- Can you access and manipulate array elements inside a function?

How to Structure Your Answer:

1. Explain how arrays are passed (by reference)
2. Describe function definition and call syntax
3. Provide an example

Sample Answer (Beginner):

"In C, arrays are passed to functions by reference. That means the function gets the address of the first element. For example:

```
void printArray(int arr[], int size) {
    for (int i = 0; i < size; i++) {
        printf("%d ", arr[i]);
    }
}
int main() {
    int nums[] = {1, 2, 3, 4, 5};
    printArray(nums, 5);
    return 0;
}
```

The array is passed without copying all the data."

Sample Answer (Experienced):

"In C, when you pass an array to a function, you're actually passing a pointer to its first element. The function definition uses either of these forms:

```
void process(int arr[], int size);
// or
void process(int *arr, int size);
```

Inside the function, you can access the elements using indexing (`arr[i]`). Multi-dimensional arrays require you to specify all but the first dimension. Since arrays are passed by reference, changes made inside the function affect the original array."

Beginner Tip:

Always pass the array size separately, as the function can't determine it automatically.

Final Thought:

Passing arrays to functions enables flexible and modular code design. Understanding pointer semantics is key to using this feature effectively.

Interview Question 34: What Are Strings in C?

Why This Question Is Asked:

Strings are essential for handling text in programs. Interviewers ask this to test your understanding of character arrays and string manipulation in C.

What the Interviewer Wants to Know:

- Do you know how strings are represented in C?
- Can you declare, initialize, and manipulate strings?
- Are you familiar with common string handling functions?

How to Structure Your Answer:

1. Define what a string is in C
2. Describe how it's stored and accessed
3. Mention string functions and give examples

Sample Answer (Beginner):

"In C, a string is an array of characters ending with a null character (\0).
Example:

```
char name[] = "John";
```

This creates a 5-character array ('J', 'o', 'h', 'n', \0)."

Sample Answer (Experienced):

"A string in C is a sequence of characters stored in a character array and
terminated with a null character ('\0'). Strings can be declared in two
ways:

```
char str1[] = "Hello";
char str2[6] = {'H','e','l','l','o','\0'};
```

C provides the <string.h> library with functions like strlen(),
strcpy(), strcmp(), and strcat() for common operations. Unlike
other languages, strings in C do not have a built-in type, so managing
memory and null-termination is critical."

Beginner Tip:

Always ensure strings are null-terminated ('\0') to avoid memory errors.

Final Thought:

Understanding strings in C is key to working with text, files, and user
input. Proper handling ensures efficient and safe programs.

Interview Question 35: How Do You Declare a String?

Why This Question Is Asked:

Declaring strings is a foundational skill for handling text in C programs. Interviewers ask this to evaluate your understanding of memory allocation and string representation.

What the Interviewer Wants to Know:

- Can you correctly declare strings in C?
- Do you understand the role of the null terminator \0?
- Are you familiar with different declaration methods?

How to Structure Your Answer:

1. Explain what a string is in C
2. Describe different ways to declare strings
3. Provide code examples for each

Sample Answer (Beginner):

"In C, a string is declared as a character array. There are two main ways to declare a string:

```
char name1[] = "Alice";              // implicit null-
termination
char name2[6] = {'A','l','i','c','e','\0'}; // explicit
declaration
```

Both declare a 6-element array with the last character being the null terminator (\0)."

Sample Answer (Experienced):

"To declare a string in C, you use a char array. There are two primary approaches:

1. **String literal (automatic null-termination):**

```c
char city[] = "Dhaka";
```

2. **Manual character array (with explicit null character):**

```c
char city[6] = {'D','h','a','k','a','\0'};
```

The size should always accommodate the null character. Declaring strings properly is essential for safe string manipulation and avoiding buffer overflows."

Beginner Tip:

Use string literals for simplicity, but remember they are automatically null-terminated.

Final Thought:

Proper string declaration ensures that text operations behave correctly and safely, especially when using string functions from `<string.h>`.

Interview Question 36: What Are Common String Functions?

Why This Question Is Asked:

C does not have a native string type, so functions in `<string.h>` are vital for string manipulation. Interviewers ask this to assess your familiarity with essential operations on character arrays.

What the Interviewer Wants to Know:

*   Can you name and describe standard string functions in C?
*   Do you know how they are used in practice?
*   Are you aware of their syntax and limitations?

How to Structure Your Answer:

1. Mention the header file required (`<string.h>`)
2. List and describe commonly used string functions
3. Give example code where appropriate

Sample Answer (Beginner):

"C provides several string functions in the `<string.h>` library. Some common ones are:

- `strlen(str)` – returns the length of the string
- `strcpy(dest, src)` – copies one string to another
- `strcmp(str1, str2)` – compares two strings
- `strcat(dest, src)` – appends one string to another
- `strchr(str, ch)` – finds the first occurrence of a character in a string"

Sample Answer (Experienced):

"The C standard library `<string.h>` provides various functions for string manipulation:

- `strlen(s)` – returns the number of characters before the null terminator
- `strcpy(dest, src)` – copies src into dest (no bounds checking)
- `strncpy(dest, src, n)` – copies up to n characters
- `strcmp(s1, s2)` – returns 0 if strings are equal, negative/positive otherwise
- `strcat(dest, src)` – appends src to the end of dest
- `strstr(haystack, needle)` – finds the substring Always be cautious with buffer sizes to avoid overflows."

Beginner Tip:

Always ensure destination arrays are large enough when using `strcpy()` or `strcat()`.

Final Thought:

Mastering string functions is essential for building interactive and user-friendly programs. Proper usage prevents bugs and memory issues.

Interview Question 37: What Is the Difference Between gets() and scanf()?

Why This Question Is Asked:

Understanding input functions is critical for safe and effective user interaction in C. Interviewers ask this to evaluate your grasp of input methods and potential vulnerabilities.

What the Interviewer Wants to Know:

- Do you understand how `gets()` and `scanf()` work?
- Can you explain their differences in usage and safety?
- Are you aware of best practices for string input?

How to Structure Your Answer:

1. Define both functions
2. Explain how they differ in reading input
3. Highlight safety and usage concerns

Sample Answer (Beginner):

"`scanf()` reads input based on a format specifier, and stops at spaces. `gets()` reads an entire line including spaces until a newline is encountered."

Sample Answer (Experienced):

"The key difference is in how they handle whitespace and input length:

- `scanf("%s", str)` reads input until the first space. It cannot read strings with spaces.
- `gets(str)` reads an entire line including spaces until a newline character. However, `gets()` is **unsafe** because it doesn't perform bounds checking, leading to buffer overflows. As a result, `gets()` has been removed from the C11 standard. `fgets()` is a safer alternative:

```
fgets(str, sizeof(str), stdin);
```

Always preferfgets()` for reading full lines."

Beginner Tip:

Avoid `gets()` and use `fgets()` instead to prevent buffer overflows.

Final Thought:

Input handling is critical to both user experience and program security. Understanding the difference between `scanf()`, `gets()`, and `fgets()` is key to writing robust C programs.

Interview Question 38: How Do You Compare Two Strings?

Why This Question Is Asked:

String comparison is a common operation in programming. Interviewers ask this to assess your understanding of how string values are compared in C.

What the Interviewer Wants to Know:

- Can you correctly compare strings in C?
- Do you know which function to use?
- Are you aware that == does not compare string content in C?

How to Structure Your Answer:

1. Explain why == doesn't work for strings
2. Introduce and explain the `strcmp()` function
3. Provide example usage

Sample Answer (Beginner):

"In C, you can't use == to compare strings because it compares memory addresses. To compare the actual content, you use the `strcmp()` function from `<string.h>`."

Sample Answer (Experienced):

"To compare two strings in C, use the `strcmp()` function from `<string.h>`. It returns:

- 0 if the strings are equal
- A positive value if the first string is greater
- A negative value if the first string is less

Example:

```c
#include <stdio.h>
#include <string.h>

int main() {
    char str1[] = "hello";
    char str2[] = "world";

    if (strcmp(str1, str2) == 0) {
        printf("Strings are equal\n");
    } else {
        printf("Strings are different\n");
    }
    return 0;
}
```

Avoid using == because it compares pointers, not string content."

Beginner Tip:

Use `strcmp()` or `strncmp()` (for limited comparisons) instead of ==.

Final Thought:

Correct string comparison is essential for writing reliable conditions in C. Knowing the difference between comparing content and memory addresses is key.

Interview Question 39: What Is a Null-Terminated String?

Why This Question Is Asked:

Null-termination is fundamental to how C handles strings. Interviewers ask this to test your understanding of string representation and memory boundaries in C.

What the Interviewer Wants to Know:

- Can you define a null-terminated string?
- Do you know how it affects string manipulation?
- Can you explain the role of the \0 character?

How to Structure Your Answer:

1. Define what a null-terminated string is
2. Describe how it is declared and used
3. Explain why the null terminator is important

Sample Answer (Beginner):

"A null-terminated string in C is a character array that ends with the special character \0. This null character tells the program where the string ends."

Sample Answer (Experienced):

"In C, a null-terminated string is an array of characters ending with a null character ('\0'). This terminator allows string functions like strlen(), strcpy(), and printf() to detect the end of the string. Without it, the program may read beyond the intended length, causing undefined behavior.

Example:

```
char str[] = "Hello";
```

This is automatically stored as { 'H', 'e', 'l', 'l', 'o', '\0'}. The null terminator is crucial for safely traversing and manipulating strings in C."

Beginner Tip:

Don't forget to allocate space for the null terminator when declaring strings manually.

Final Thought:

Null-terminated strings are the foundation of text handling in C. Mismanaging them can lead to serious bugs, so understanding their structure is essential.

Interview Question 40: What Are Character Arrays?

Why This Question Is Asked:

Character arrays are fundamental to string manipulation in C. Interviewers ask this to assess your understanding of how text is stored and processed at a low level.

What the Interviewer Wants to Know:

- Can you define a character array?
- Do you understand how it's used to store strings?
- Can you describe how it differs from string objects in higher-level languages?

How to Structure Your Answer:

1. Define what a character array is
2. Describe its relationship with strings in C
3. Provide examples of declaration and use

Sample Answer (Beginner):

"A character array is a collection of characters stored in contiguous memory locations. In C, strings are usually stored as character arrays ending with a null character (\0)."

Sample Answer (Experienced):

"In C, a character array is a sequence of characters stored in memory, used to represent strings. Unlike languages with built-in string types, C uses char arrays for string operations. For example:

```
char name[] = "Alice";
```

This is equivalent to:

```
char name[6] = {'A', 'l', 'i', 'c', 'e', '\0'};
```

The null character ('\0') marks the end of the string. Character arrays allow direct memory access and manipulation, which is powerful but requires careful handling."

Beginner Tip:

Character arrays must be null-terminated to be used as strings in standard library functions.

Final Thought:

Understanding character arrays is key to mastering strings and memory in C. They are simple yet powerful tools for low-level text processing.

Interview Question 41: How Is Memory Allocated to Strings?

Why This Question Is Asked:
Memory management is crucial in C, especially with strings that are essentially character arrays. Interviewers ask this to evaluate your understanding of memory allocation, both static and dynamic.

What the Interviewer Wants to Know:

- Do you understand how strings are stored in memory?
- Can you explain static vs. dynamic allocation for strings?
- Are you aware of null terminator importance in allocation?

How to Structure Your Answer:

1. Explain static memory allocation for strings
2. Explain dynamic memory allocation using pointers
3. Mention the null terminator requirement

Sample Answer (Beginner):

"Memory for strings in C can be allocated at compile-time when using character arrays:

```
char str[6] = "Hello"; // 5 characters + 1 for null
terminator
```

This allocates a fixed-size block of memory."

Sample Answer (Experienced):

"In C, string memory can be allocated in two ways:

- **Static Allocation**:

```
char name[] = "John"; // Allocates 5 bytes including
'\0'
```

- **Dynamic Allocation**:

```
char *name = (char *)malloc(20 * sizeof(char));
```

This reserves 20 bytes at runtime. Always ensure you allocate space for the null terminator ('\0'). Also, free dynamically allocated memory using free(name); to avoid memory leaks."

Beginner Tip:

Always account for the null terminator when allocating memory manually.

Final Thought:

Proper string memory allocation ensures safe and efficient program behavior. Failing to allocate enough space, especially for the null terminator, can lead to bugs and security issues.

Interview Question 42: What Is Buffer Overflow?

Why This Question Is Asked:

Buffer overflows are a common and dangerous security issue in C programs. Interviewers ask this to assess your awareness of memory safety and secure coding practices.

What the Interviewer Wants to Know:

- Can you define what a buffer overflow is?
- Do you understand how and why it happens?
- Are you familiar with how to prevent it?

How to Structure Your Answer:

1. Define buffer overflow
2. Explain how it occurs in C (especially with arrays and strings)
3. Provide examples and mention prevention techniques

Sample Answer (Beginner):

"A buffer overflow happens when more data is written to a buffer (like an array) than it can hold. This can overwrite nearby memory and crash the program."

Sample Answer (Experienced):

"Buffer overflow is a condition where a program writes data beyond the boundaries of allocated memory. In C, it commonly occurs with arrays or strings:

```
char str[5];
strcpy(str, "abcdef"); // Overwrites memory beyond str
```

This can corrupt data, crash the program, or even allow attackers to inject malicious code. It's a major source of security vulnerabilities. Prevention techniques include:

- Using safe functions like `strncpy()` or `fgets()`
- Always allocating space for the null terminator
- Performing bounds checking
- Using modern tools like AddressSanitizer and compiler flags (`-fstack-protector`)"

Beginner Tip:

Avoid `gets()` and always verify the size of input when using `scanf()` or `strcpy()`.

Final Thought:

Understanding and preventing buffer overflows is vital for secure C programming. It protects your programs from crashes, data corruption, and security breaches.

Interview Question 43: How Do You Reverse a String in C?

Why This Question Is Asked:

String reversal is a classic programming challenge. Interviewers ask this to evaluate your logic-building skills, string manipulation techniques, and knowledge of character arrays.

What the Interviewer Wants to Know:

- Can you manipulate character arrays effectively?
- Do you understand string length and indexing?
- Can you implement logic using loops or pointers?

How to Structure Your Answer:
1. Describe the goal and the logic
2. Explain the loop or pointer-based approach
3. Provide a sample implementation

Sample Answer (Beginner):
"To reverse a string in C, I use a loop to swap characters from the start and end of the string until I reach the middle."

Sample Answer (Experienced):
"Here's one way to reverse a string using a two-pointer approach:

```c
#include <stdio.h>
#include <string.h>

void reverse(char str[]) {
    int start = 0;
    int end = strlen(str) - 1;
    while (start < end) {
        char temp = str[start];
        str[start] = str[end];
        str[end] = temp;
        start++;
        end--;
    }
}

int main() {
    char str[] = "hello";
    reverse(str);
    printf("Reversed string: %s\n", str);
    return 0;
}
```

This function works by swapping characters at opposite ends, moving toward the center."

Beginner Tip:

Remember that strings must be null-terminated (\0) for functions like `strlen()` to work correctly.

Final Thought:

Reversing a string strengthens your grasp of loops, indices, and memory in C. It's a great practice problem for mastering character arrays.

Interview Question 44: What Are Pointers to Strings?

Why This Question Is Asked:

Pointers to strings are frequently used in C due to the language's low-level memory model. Interviewers ask this to assess your understanding of string handling, pointers, and memory referencing.

What the Interviewer Wants to Know:

- Can you define what a pointer to a string is?
- Do you understand how it's different from a character array?
- Can you use and manipulate string pointers properly?

How to Structure Your Answer:

1. Define pointers to strings
2. Compare them with character arrays
3. Provide usage examples and explain benefits

Sample Answer (Beginner):

"A pointer to a string in C is a pointer to the first character of a string. It's usually declared like `char *str = "Hello";`."

"In C, a pointer to a string refers to a pointer that holds the address of the first character in a null-terminated character array. For example:

```
char *greet = "Hello";
```

This stores the address of the string literal "Hello". Unlike `char arr[] = "Hello";`, where the characters are stored in a modifiable array, `char *str = "Hello";` points to a string literal, which is typically stored in read-only memory and should not be modified.

Pointers to strings are useful when passing strings to functions or managing dynamic memory. You can access characters using indexing (`str[i]`) or pointer arithmetic (`*(str + i)`)."

Beginner Tip:

Don't try to modify string literals through a `char *` pointer. Use `char[]` if you need a modifiable string.

Final Thought:

Understanding pointers to strings is key to efficient and safe string handling in C. It's a fundamental concept for mastering memory and function communication.

Interview Question 45: Difference Between Array of Characters and Pointer to Characters?

Why This Question Is Asked:

Understanding the difference between character arrays and character pointers is crucial for string manipulation and memory management. Interviewers ask this to evaluate your grasp of low-level data handling in C.

What the Interviewer Wants to Know:

- Do you understand how character arrays and character pointers differ?
- Can you explain how memory is allocated and accessed?
- Are you aware of mutability and safety considerations?

How to Structure Your Answer:

1. Define character arrays and character pointers
2. Compare memory storage and mutability
3. Provide usage examples and implications

Sample Answer (Beginner):

"A character array stores characters in a block of memory and can be modified. A pointer to a character points to a string literal, which is usually read-only."

Sample Answer (Experienced):

"The difference lies in storage, mutability, and memory access:

- **Character Array**:

```
char str1[] = "Hello";
```

This allocates a modifiable array of 6 characters (`'H'`,`'e'`,`'l'`,`'l'`,`'o'`,`'\0'`) on the stack.

- **Pointer to Character**:

```
char *str2 = "Hello";
```

This points to a string literal stored in read-only memory. Modifying `str2[0]` is undefined behavior.

Key Differences:

- Arrays allocate space, pointers reference space.
- Arrays are mutable, string literals (pointed by char *) are not.
- You can use sizeof(str1) to get total array size, but not with str2.

Beginner Tip:

Use char[] if you need to modify the string, and char * for read-only access to string literals.

Final Thought:

Understanding this distinction prevents memory errors and makes your string-handling code in C safer and more predictable.

Interview Question 46: What Is the Difference Between strlen() and sizeof()?

Why This Question Is Asked:

This is a common question to test your understanding of memory usage and data size in C. It reveals how well you grasp the distinction between actual content length and allocated memory size.

What the Interviewer Wants to Know:

- Do you understand what each function does?
- Can you explain their outputs in the context of strings?
- Are you aware of their scope and limitations?

How to Structure Your Answer:

1. Define strlen() and sizeof() individually
2. Compare their behavior when used on strings
3. Provide code examples to illustrate

Sample Answer (Beginner):

"`strlen()` returns the number of characters in a string, not counting the null terminator. `sizeof()` returns the total memory allocated, including the null character if it's an array."

Sample Answer (Experienced):

"`strlen()` is a function from `<string.h>` that calculates the length of a string (number of characters before the null terminator \0). It must traverse the string to count characters:

```
strlen("Hello") // returns 5
```

`sizeof()` is an operator evaluated at compile time that gives the total memory size in bytes of a variable or data type:

```
char str[] = "Hello";
sizeof(str) // returns 6 (5 characters + '\0')
```

However, if used on a pointer:

```
char *ptr = "Hello";
sizeof(ptr) // returns 4 or 8 (size of pointer, not
string)
```

Key Differences:
- `strlen()` counts characters at runtime.
- `sizeof()` gives allocated size at compile time.
- `sizeof()` on pointers returns pointer size, not content size.

Beginner Tip:
Use `strlen()` to measure string content, and `sizeof()` for memory-related calculations.

Final Thought:

Understanding the distinction between `strlen()` and `sizeof()` is essential for proper memory handling and debugging in C.

Interview Question 47: How Do You Concatenate Strings?

Why This Question Is Asked:

String concatenation is a common operation in C. Interviewers ask this to check your knowledge of string manipulation, memory handling, and use of standard library functions.

What the Interviewer Wants to Know:

- Do you understand how to safely join two strings?
- Can you use strcat() and strncat() correctly?
- Are you aware of the importance of memory limits?

How to Structure Your Answer:
1. Explain what string concatenation means
2. Describe how it's done in C using functions
3. Provide examples and warnings

Sample Answer (Beginner):
"To concatenate two strings in C, I use the strcat() function from the <string.h> library. It appends one string to the end of another."

Sample Answer (Experienced):
"In C, string concatenation is done using strcat() or strncat() from <string.h>. Example:

```
#include <stdio.h>
#include <string.h>

int main() {
    char str1[20] = "Hello ";
    char str2[] = "World!";
    strcat(str1, str2);
    printf("%s\n", str1);
    return 0;
}
```

This appends `str2` to `str1`. Ensure `str1` has enough space to hold the combined result, including the null terminator. `strncat()` adds a safety limit:

```
strncat(str1, str2, sizeof(str1) - strlen(str1) - 1);
```

Beginner Tip:

Always allocate enough space in the destination string before concatenating.

Final Thought:

Proper string concatenation in C requires careful attention to memory size and null-termination. Using safe alternatives like `strncat()` helps avoid buffer overflows.

Interview Question 48: What Is the Use of `strcpy()` and `strncpy()`?

Why This Question Is Asked:

String copying is a frequent task in C. Interviewers ask this to evaluate your knowledge of standard library functions, memory safety, and string handling best practices.

What the Interviewer Wants to Know:

- Do you know how `strcpy()` and `strncpy()` work?
- Can you explain their syntax and risks?
- Are you aware of when to use which function?

How to Structure Your Answer:

1. Define what each function does
2. Highlight their syntax and behavior
3. Compare them and explain when to use which

Sample Answer (Beginner):

"`strcpy()` copies one string to another. `strncpy()` is a safer version that limits the number of characters copied."

Sample Answer (Experienced):

"In C, `strcpy()` and `strncpy()` are used to copy strings from a source to a destination:

- `strcpy(dest, src)` copies the null-terminated string from `src` to `dest`. It does not perform bounds checking, so it can lead to buffer overflows.
- `strncpy(dest, src, n)` copies up to n characters from `src`. If `src` is shorter than n, the rest is padded with null characters. It helps prevent overflows but may not null-terminate if `src` is longer.

Example:

```
char dest[10];
strcpy(dest, "Hi");
strncpy(dest, "HelloWorld", 9); // leaves space for
null terminator
```

Key Differences:

- `strcpy()` is faster but unsafe if the destination size is unknown.
- `strncpy()` adds control but needs careful null-termination handling.

Beginner Tip:

Use `strncpy()` when the size of the destination buffer is limited, but always manually null-terminate if needed.

Final Thought:

Choosing the right function is vital for memory safety. Prefer `strncpy()` in production code, and consider `snprintf()` or safer wrappers for better control.

Interview Question 49: How Do You Count Characters or Words in a String?

Why This Question Is Asked:

Counting characters and words in strings is a common task in text processing. Interviewers ask this to assess your skills in string traversal, logic-building, and use of standard functions.

What the Interviewer Wants to Know:

- Do you know how to traverse a string in C?
- Can you write logic to count specific elements (like characters or words)?
- Are you aware of the use of whitespace in word separation?

How to Structure Your Answer:

1. Explain how to count characters using `strlen()` or a loop
2. Explain how to count words using logic for space or delimiter detection
3. Provide example code

Sample Answer (Beginner):

"To count characters, I use `strlen()` which returns the number of characters before the null terminator. To count words, I count how many spaces there are and add 1."

Sample Answer (Experienced):

"Characters can be counted using:

```
int count = strlen(str);
```

Words can be counted by iterating through the string and counting transitions from a non-word to a word character. Example:

```c
int countWords(const char *str) {
    int count = 0, inWord = 0;
    while (*str) {
        if (*str != ' ' && *str != '\n' && *str !=
'\t') {
            if (!inWord) {
                count++;
                inWord = 1;
            }
        } else {
            inWord = 0;
        }
        str++;
    }
    return count;
}
```

This handles multiple spaces and tabs between words."

Beginner Tip:

Don't count spaces directly as words—use logic to detect transitions between whitespace and characters.

Final Thought:

String traversal is a core C skill. Accurate counting of characters and words strengthens your foundation in text processing and algorithmic thinking.

Interview Question 50: How Do You Handle Strings Without Using Library Functions?

Why This Question Is Asked:

Interviewers ask this to evaluate your understanding of string fundamentals in C, particularly your ability to implement string operations manually using pointers and arrays.

What the Interviewer Wants to Know:

- Can you manipulate strings at the character level?
- Do you understand how functions like `strlen()`, `strcpy()`, etc., work internally?
- Can you write efficient, bug-free custom logic?

How to Structure Your Answer:

1. State why manual string handling may be needed (e.g., learning, embedded systems)
2. Explain how you can implement common operations like length, copy, compare, etc.
3. Provide code examples for at least one operation

Sample Answer (Beginner):

"If I can't use library functions, I can still handle strings by treating them as character arrays. For example, I can count characters using a loop until I reach the null terminator."

Sample Answer (Experienced):

"Handling strings manually means implementing functions like `strlen()`, `strcpy()`, and `strcmp()` yourself. Example:

```
int my_strlen(const char *str) {
    int len = 0;
    while (str[len] != '\0') {
        len++;
    }
    return len;
}

void my_strcpy(char *dest, const char *src) {
    while (*src) {
        *dest++ = *src++;
    }
    *dest = '\0';
}
```

This approach requires careful memory handling, especially to avoid buffer overflows. It's a good way to learn how strings work under the hood."

Beginner Tip:

 Always terminate your manually copied string with a \0 to prevent undefined behavior.

Final Thought:

 Working with strings manually builds a deep understanding of C's memory model. It's also valuable in restricted environments where standard libraries may not be available.

Section 3: Pointers & Memory Management (51–75)

Interview Question 51: What Is a Pointer?

Why This Question Is Asked:

 Pointers are one of the most powerful and essential concepts in C programming. Interviewers ask this to assess your understanding of memory access, variable referencing, and low-level data manipulation.

What the Interviewer Wants to Know:

- Can you clearly define what a pointer is?
- Do you understand how pointers interact with memory?
- Can you use pointers in basic operations and explain their syntax?

How to Structure Your Answer:

1. Define a pointer and explain its purpose
2. Describe pointer declaration and usage
3. Provide examples and highlight benefits

Sample Answer (Beginner):

"A pointer is a variable that stores the memory address of another variable. In C, pointers help with dynamic memory, arrays, and function arguments."

Sample Answer (Experienced):

"In C, a pointer is a variable that holds the address of another variable. It is declared using an asterisk (*). Example:

```
int x = 10;
int *ptr = &x; // ptr points to x
```

Here, &x gets the address of x, and *ptr accesses the value stored at that address (10).

Pointers are used for:

- Dynamic memory management
- Efficient array and string handling
- Function argument passing by reference

Understanding pointers is key to mastering C programming."

Beginner Tip:

Don't confuse * for declaration (int *p) and dereferencing (*p = 5).

Final Thought:

Pointers provide direct memory access, enabling powerful programming techniques. However, they must be handled carefully to avoid segmentation faults and memory leaks.

Interview Question 52: How Do You Declare and Use Pointers?

Why This Question Is Asked:

Pointer declaration and usage are fundamental to C programming. Interviewers ask this to test your practical knowledge of pointers, memory referencing, and data access.

What the Interviewer Wants to Know:

- Can you declare and initialize a pointer correctly?
- Do you understand how to access and modify values through pointers?
- Are you familiar with pointer syntax and best practices?

How to Structure Your Answer:

1. Explain how to declare a pointer
2. Describe how to assign and dereference pointers
3. Provide working examples

Sample Answer (Beginner):

"To declare a pointer, I use an asterisk (*) before the pointer name. I assign it the address of a variable using the address-of operator (&), and access the value using dereferencing (*)."

Sample Answer (Experienced):

"Pointers are declared with an asterisk (*) to indicate that the variable holds a memory address:

```
int num = 10;
int *ptr = &num; // ptr holds the address of num
```

You can access and modify the value using dereferencing:

```
*ptr = 20; // changes num to 20
```

You can also use pointers in function parameters to modify values outside the function scope. This is known as call by reference."

Beginner Tip:

Initialize pointers before using them, and avoid dereferencing null or uninitialized pointers.

Final Thought:

Correct declaration and use of pointers are crucial for efficient and error-free C programming. Mastery of pointers unlocks advanced memory and data manipulation techniques.

Interview Question 53: What Is the Use of the * and & Operators?

Why This Question Is Asked:

Understanding * and & is essential for working with pointers in C. Interviewers ask this to test your grasp of memory addressing and value referencing.

What the Interviewer Wants to Know:

- Do you know what * and & do in the context of pointers?
- Can you explain how they are used together?
- Are you aware of common mistakes and best practices?

How to Structure Your Answer:

1. Define the role of * (dereference operator)
2. Define the role of & (address-of operator)
3. Provide clear examples of how both are used

Sample Answer (Beginner):

"In C, & is used to get the address of a variable, and * is used to get the value stored at a memory address (dereferencing a pointer)."

Sample Answer (Experienced):

"The & operator is the **address-of** operator. It returns the memory address of a variable:

```
int x = 10;
int *p = &x; // p now holds the address of x
```

The * operator is the **dereference** operator. It accesses the value stored at the memory location pointed to by a pointer:

```
*p = 20; // changes x to 20
```

Together, * and & are used to pass values by reference and manipulate memory directly."

Beginner Tip:

Remember: * declares a pointer or accesses a value, while & gets the address of a variable.

Final Thought:

Mastering * and & is foundational for understanding pointers, dynamic memory, and function arguments in C.

Interview Question 54: What Is a NULL Pointer?

Why This Question Is Asked:

NULL pointers are a critical concept in C to signify that a pointer doesn't point to a valid memory location. Interviewers ask this to test your understanding of pointer safety and error handling.

What the Interviewer Wants to Know:

- Do you know what a NULL pointer is and when to use it?
- Can you explain how to declare and check a NULL pointer?
- Are you aware of the dangers of dereferencing NULL pointers?

How to Structure Your Answer:

1. Define a NULL pointer and its purpose
2. Show how to declare and use one
3. Mention common use cases and precautions

Sample Answer (Beginner):

"A NULL pointer is a pointer that doesn't point to any memory location. It is used to indicate that the pointer is not currently assigned."

Sample Answer (Experienced):

"In C, a NULL pointer is one that has been assigned the value NULL to indicate it points to nothing:

```
int *ptr = NULL;
```

It's useful for:

- Initializing pointers before assigning valid addresses
- Checking if a pointer is assigned
- Signaling errors or end-of-data in functions

Dereferencing a NULL pointer causes a runtime error (segmentation fault). Always check if a pointer is NULL before accessing it:

```
if (ptr != NULL) {
    // safe to use *ptr
}
```

"

Beginner Tip:
Use NULL when declaring pointers until they are assigned a valid address.
Final Thought:

Using NULL pointers safely helps prevent crashes and undefined behavior. It's an essential practice in robust C programming.

Interview Question 55: What Is Pointer Arithmetic?

Why This Question Is Asked:

Pointer arithmetic is a unique and powerful feature in C. Interviewers ask this to evaluate your understanding of how pointers interact with memory and arrays.

What the Interviewer Wants to Know:

- Can you explain how arithmetic operations work on pointers?
- Do you understand how pointer arithmetic relates to memory addressing?
- Can you use it safely and correctly?

How to Structure Your Answer:

1. Define pointer arithmetic and when it's used
2. Describe how addition, subtraction, and comparison work with pointers
3. Provide examples with arrays or memory addresses

Sample Answer (Beginner):

"Pointer arithmetic means performing operations like addition or subtraction on pointers. It helps move from one memory address to another, especially in arrays."

Sample Answer (Experienced):

"Pointer arithmetic refers to modifying the memory address stored in a pointer. In C, you can:

- Add an integer to a pointer (ptr + n) to move forward n elements
- Subtract an integer from a pointer (ptr - n) to move backward
- Subtract two pointers to find the number of elements between them

Example:

```
int arr[] = {10, 20, 30, 40};
int *p = arr;
printf("%d\n", *(p + 2)); // outputs 30
```

Here, p + 2 moves the pointer two elements forward in the array.

Pointer arithmetic respects data type sizes, so adding 1 to an int * actually adds sizeof(int) bytes."

Beginner Tip:

Use pointer arithmetic mainly with arrays or dynamically allocated memory, and always stay within bounds.

Final Thought:

Pointer arithmetic is efficient but risky. It gives you powerful control over memory, but you must use it with caution to avoid accessing invalid locations.

Interview Question 56: How Do You Pass Pointers to Functions?

Why This Question Is Asked:

Passing pointers to functions enables direct memory manipulation and allows changes to variables outside the function. Interviewers ask this to assess your understanding of function calls and reference-based programming in C.

What the Interviewer Wants to Know:

- Do you know how to declare and use pointer parameters in functions?
- Can you explain how passing pointers enables modifying original values?
- Are you aware of syntax and safety considerations?

How to Structure Your Answer:

1. Explain how pointers can be passed to functions
2. Describe the syntax and behavior
3. Provide a working example

Sample Answer (Beginner):

"You can pass a pointer to a function to allow it to change the value of a variable outside the function."

Sample Answer (Experienced):

"To pass a pointer to a function, declare the parameter as a pointer in the function definition:

```
void update(int *p) {
    *p = *p + 10;
}

int main() {
    int x = 5;
    update(&x);
    printf("%d\n", x); // prints 15
    return 0;
}
```

This allows the function to directly modify the value of x through its address. It's commonly used for modifying variables, returning multiple values, and handling large data efficiently."

Beginner Tip:
Always check that a pointer is not NULL before using it inside a function.
Final Thought:
Passing pointers to functions makes your code more efficient and flexible. It's a core technique in C for handling arrays, dynamic memory, and inter-function communication.

Interview Question 57: What Is a Pointer to Pointer?

Why This Question Is Asked:

Pointers to pointers are used in advanced C programming for dynamic memory allocation, arrays of strings, and handling multidimensional arrays. Interviewers ask this to assess your deeper understanding of pointer manipulation.

What the Interviewer Wants to Know:

- Can you define and explain a pointer to a pointer?
- Do you understand how to declare, dereference, and use it?
- Can you apply this knowledge in real scenarios like `malloc()` or string arrays?

How to Structure Your Answer:

1. Define what a pointer to pointer is
2. Explain how it's declared and used
3. Provide code examples and practical applications

Sample Answer (Beginner):

"A pointer to a pointer stores the address of another pointer. It allows us to access and modify pointer values indirectly."

Sample Answer (Experienced):

"A pointer to a pointer (e.g., `int **ptr`) is a variable that holds the address of another pointer. Example:

```
int x = 10;
int *p = &x;
int **pp = &p;

printf("%d\n", **pp); // prints 10
```

This is useful in:

- Dynamic memory allocation with double pointers (e.g., `int **arr = malloc(n * sizeof(int *));`)
- Passing a pointer to a function to modify it (like `char **argv` in `main()`)
- Working with arrays of strings

Each level of * lets you access a deeper level of indirection."

Beginner Tip:

Each * means another level of indirection. *ptr gets the value, **ptr digs one level deeper.

Final Thought:

Pointers to pointers enable powerful techniques in C, especially for managing complex data structures like arrays, matrices, and dynamic references.

Interview Question 58: What Is a Function Pointer?

Why This Question Is Asked:

Function pointers allow dynamic selection and invocation of functions, which is useful for callbacks, implementing function tables, and writing flexible code. Interviewers ask this to test your understanding of advanced pointer usage in C.

What the Interviewer Wants to Know:

- Do you understand what a function pointer is?
- Can you declare, assign, and call a function through a pointer?
- Do you know practical use cases for function pointers?

How to Structure Your Answer:

1. Define what a function pointer is
2. Show how to declare and assign one
3. Provide usage examples and mention use cases

Sample Answer (Beginner):

"A function pointer is a pointer that stores the address of a function. You can call the function using the pointer."

Sample Answer (Experienced):

"A function pointer holds the address of a function and allows calling the function dynamically. Syntax:

```
void greet() {
    printf("Hello!\n");
}

void (*funcPtr)() = greet;
funcPtr(); // Calls greet()
```

Function pointers are used in:

- Callback mechanisms (like signal handlers)
- Passing behavior to functions (e.g., sorting with `qsort()`)
- Implementing function tables or state machines

You must match the pointer type exactly with the function signature."

Beginner Tip:
Use parentheses when declaring function pointers: `returnType (*ptrName)(parameterTypes);`

Final Thought:
Function pointers add flexibility and power to C programs. They are essential for implementing callbacks, plugins, and abstracting behaviors.

Interview Question 59: What Are Wild Pointers?

Why This Question Is Asked:

Wild pointers are a common source of bugs and undefined behavior in C.
Interviewers ask this to evaluate your understanding of pointer
initialization and safe memory practices.

What the Interviewer Wants to Know:

- Can you define a wild pointer?
- Do you know how they occur?
- Can you explain how to avoid them?

How to Structure Your Answer:

1. Define what a wild pointer is
2. Explain how wild pointers are created
3. Describe how to prevent and handle them safely

Sample Answer (Beginner):

"A wild pointer is a pointer that has not been initialized. It may point to
any random memory location."

Sample Answer (Experienced):

"A wild pointer is an uninitialized pointer that points to an unknown or
random memory location. Using a wild pointer leads to undefined
behavior, memory corruption, or crashes. Example:

```
int *ptr;    // uninitialized - wild pointer
*ptr = 10;   // undefined behavior
```

Wild pointers often arise from:

- Declaration without initialization
- Using freed memory without resetting the pointer

To avoid wild pointers:

- Always initialize pointers, e.g., `int *ptr = NULL;`
- Set pointers to NULL after freeing them
- Check if a pointer is NULL before dereferencing

Beginner Tip:

Avoid using a pointer until it's initialized to a valid address or explicitly set to NULL.

Final Thought:

Wild pointers are dangerous and hard to debug. Proper initialization and defensive coding help avoid critical runtime issues.

Interview Question 60: What Is a Memory Leak?

Why This Question Is Asked:

Memory leaks lead to inefficient memory usage and can crash long-running programs. Interviewers ask this to test your understanding of dynamic memory and resource management in C.

What the Interviewer Wants to Know:

- Can you define what a memory leak is?
- Do you understand how and why it happens?
- Can you explain how to detect and prevent it?

How to Structure Your Answer:
1. Define a memory leak
2. Explain how it occurs in C
3. Provide prevention and detection techniques

Sample Answer (Beginner):
"A memory leak happens when a program allocates memory but forgets to free it. Over time, this can use up all the system's memory."

Sample Answer (Experienced):

"In C, a memory leak occurs when dynamically allocated memory is not freed using `free()`, and the pointer to that memory is lost. Example:

```
int *ptr = malloc(sizeof(int) * 10);
// ptr is reassigned or the function returns without
freeing
```

The allocated memory remains in use but inaccessible, leading to wasted resources.

To prevent memory leaks:

- Always pair `malloc()` or `calloc()` with `free()`
- Use tools like Valgrind to detect memory leaks
- Set pointers to NULL after freeing them to avoid dangling references"

Beginner Tip:

Track every dynamic allocation and ensure each is freed before program exit.

Final Thought:

Memory leaks reduce program efficiency and can eventually crash systems. Careful memory management and debugging tools help you write leak-free programs.

Interview Question 61: How Do You Allocate Memory Dynamically?

Why This Question Is Asked:

Dynamic memory allocation is essential for building flexible and scalable programs. Interviewers ask this to evaluate your understanding of heap memory usage and memory management functions in C.

What the Interviewer Wants to Know:

- Do you know how to allocate and free memory dynamically?
- Can you correctly use functions like `malloc()`, `calloc()`, `realloc()`?
- Do you manage memory safely to prevent leaks?

How to Structure Your Answer:

1. Define what dynamic memory allocation is
2. List standard functions used (`malloc`, `calloc`, `realloc`, `free`)
3. Show examples with correct usage

Sample Answer (Beginner):

"Dynamic memory allocation allows you to allocate memory at runtime using functions like `malloc()` and `free()` to release it."

Sample Answer (Experienced):

"In C, dynamic memory is allocated on the heap using standard library functions:

- `malloc(size)` – allocates uninitialized memory
- `calloc(n, size)` – allocates zero-initialized memory for an array
- `realloc(ptr, newSize)` – resizes previously allocated memory
- `free(ptr)` – deallocates previously allocated memory

Example:

```
int *arr = (int *)malloc(5 * sizeof(int));
if (arr != NULL) {
    // use arr
    free(arr); // release memory
}
```

Always check if memory allocation was successful and free it when done."

Beginner Tip:

Always pair every `malloc` or `calloc` with `free` to prevent memory leaks.

Final Thought:

Dynamic memory allocation is powerful but requires careful management. Always check pointers, handle errors, and free memory to maintain safe and efficient code.

Interview Question 61: How Do You Allocate Memory Dynamically?

Why This Question Is Asked:

Dynamic memory allocation is essential for building flexible and scalable programs. Interviewers ask this to evaluate your understanding of heap memory usage and memory management functions in C.

What the Interviewer Wants to Know:

- Do you know how to allocate and free memory dynamically?
- Can you correctly use functions like `malloc()`, `calloc()`, `realloc()`?
- Do you manage memory safely to prevent leaks?

How to Structure Your Answer:

1. Define what dynamic memory allocation is
2. List standard functions used (`malloc`, `calloc`, `realloc`, `free`)
3. Show examples with correct usage

Sample Answer (Beginner):
"Dynamic memory allocation allows you to allocate memory at runtime using functions like `malloc()` and `free()` to release it."

Sample Answer (Experienced):

"In C, dynamic memory is allocated on the heap using standard library functions:

- `malloc(size)` – allocates uninitialized memory
- `calloc(n, size)` – allocates zero-initialized memory for an array
- `realloc(ptr, newSize)` – resizes previously allocated memory
- `free(ptr)` – deallocates previously allocated memory

Example:

```
int *arr = (int *)malloc(5 * sizeof(int));
if (arr != NULL) {
    // use arr
    free(arr); // release memory
}
```

Always check if memory allocation was successful and free it when done."

Beginner Tip:

Always pair every `malloc` or `calloc` with `free` to prevent memory leaks.

Final Thought:

Dynamic memory allocation is powerful but requires careful management. Always check pointers, handle errors, and free memory to maintain safe and efficient code.

Interview Question 63: What Is the Difference Between Stack and Heap Memory?

Why This Question Is Asked:

Understanding stack and heap memory is crucial for managing variables, memory allocation, and program performance. Interviewers ask this to test your knowledge of memory structure and allocation in C.

What the Interviewer Wants to Know:

- Can you distinguish between stack and heap memory?
- Do you know the use cases, limitations, and lifetimes of each?
- Are you aware of memory management responsibilities in each region?

How to Structure Your Answer:

1. Define stack and heap memory
2. Compare their characteristics and uses
3. Provide examples and mention key differences

Sample Answer (Beginner):

"The stack is used for static memory like local variables, and the heap is used for dynamic memory like when using `malloc()`."

Sample Answer (Experienced):

"In C, memory is divided into two major regions:

- **Stack Memory:**
  - Stores local variables and function call information
  - Automatically managed (allocated and freed by the compiler)
  - Fast access but limited in size
  - Variables are deleted once the function ends

- **Heap Memory**:
    - Used for dynamic memory allocation (`malloc()`, `calloc()`)
    - Manually managed by the programmer (requires `free()`)
    - Larger but slower than stack
    - Memory persists until explicitly deallocated

Example:

```
int x = 10;           // stored on stack
int *p = malloc(10);  // memory from heap
```

Key Differences:

- Stack is auto-managed; heap is manual
- Stack has limited size; heap is large
- Stack variables die with the function; heap variables live until freed

Beginner Tip:

Always `free()` heap memory to avoid leaks; stack memory is cleaned up automatically.

Final Thought:

Mastering stack vs. heap memory is essential for writing efficient and bug-free C programs, especially when managing large or persistent data.

Interview Question 64: What Are Dangling Pointers?

Why This Question Is Asked:

Dangling pointers are a dangerous source of bugs and crashes in C programs. Interviewers ask this to test your understanding of memory deallocation, pointer safety, and debugging skills.

What the Interviewer Wants to Know:

- Can you define a dangling pointer?
- Do you understand how and when it occurs?
- Can you explain how to avoid or fix it?

How to Structure Your Answer:

1. Define what a dangling pointer is
2. Explain how dangling pointers are created
3. Provide examples and prevention techniques

Sample Answer (Beginner):

"A dangling pointer is a pointer that still points to a memory location that has been freed or is out of scope. Using it causes undefined behavior."

Sample Answer (Experienced):

"A dangling pointer in C is a pointer that refers to a memory location which has been deallocated or is no longer valid. It occurs in cases such as:

- Returning the address of a local variable from a function:

```
int* getPtr() {
    int x = 10;
    return &x; // x goes out of scope
}
```

- Freeing heap memory but still using the pointer:

```
int *p = (int *)malloc(sizeof(int));
free(p);
*p = 5; // dangling pointer usage
```

To prevent dangling pointers:

- Set pointers to NULL after freeing memory
- Avoid returning addresses of local variables
- Use tools like Valgrind to detect such bugs

Beginner Tip:

After calling `free()`, set the pointer to NULL to ensure it doesn't point to invalid memory.

Final Thought:

Dangling pointers can lead to hard-to-find bugs. Writing safe code and being cautious with memory helps you avoid such pitfalls.

Interview Question 65: What Is the Size of a Pointer?

Why This Question Is Asked:

Knowing the size of pointers is important for understanding memory usage, architecture differences, and pointer arithmetic. Interviewers ask this to evaluate your awareness of system-level details in C.

What the Interviewer Wants to Know:

- Do you understand that the size of a pointer depends on the system architecture?
- Can you explain how it relates to memory addressing?
- Do you know how to find the size of a pointer in C?

How to Structure Your Answer:
1. Explain what determines the size of a pointer
2. Mention common pointer sizes on different systems
3. Show how to check pointer size using `sizeof()`

Sample Answer (Beginner):
"The size of a pointer depends on the system's architecture. On a 32-bit system, it's usually 4 bytes; on a 64-bit system, it's 8 bytes."

Sample Answer (Experienced):
"In C, the size of a pointer is architecture-dependent:
- 4 bytes on 32-bit systems
- 8 bytes on 64-bit systems

This is because pointers store memory addresses, and the size must match the address width of the system.

You can determine the size of a pointer using:

```
printf("%zu\n", sizeof(int *));
printf("%zu\n", sizeof(void *));
```

All pointer types (e.g., `int *`, `char *`, `float *`) usually have the same size on a given architecture, though they point to different data types.

Beginner Tip:

Always use `sizeof()` to programmatically determine pointer sizes rather than assuming a fixed size.

Final Thought:

Understanding pointer size is essential when writing portable, low-level, or memory-sensitive C programs.

Interview Question 66: What Is the Difference Between `const int *` and `int const *`?

Why This Question Is Asked:

Interviewers use this to test your understanding of const correctness and pointer syntax. It's essential for writing safe, maintainable C code.

What the Interviewer Wants to Know:

- Do you know how `const` applies to pointers?
- Can you explain the difference in intent and behavior?
- Can you provide examples?

How to Structure Your Answer:

1. Explain what `const int *` and `int const *` mean
2. Clarify that they are functionally equivalent
3. Mention where the confusion typically arises

Sample Answer (Beginner):

"Both `const int *` and `int const *` mean the same thing: the pointer points to a constant integer, so the value it points to cannot be changed."

Sample Answer (Experienced):

"In C, `const` can be written before or after the type. So:

```
const int *ptr;
int const *ptr;
```

Both declare a pointer to a constant integer. You cannot do `*ptr = 10;`.

To clarify:

- `const int *ptr` → pointer to a `const int`
- `int *const ptr` → const pointer to an `int` (you can't change the pointer, but can change the value it points to)
- `const int *const ptr` → const pointer to a `const int` (neither the pointer nor the value can be changed)

Beginner Tip:

Read pointer declarations right-to-left for clarity: `int const *` = pointer to constant int.

Final Thought:

Understanding the placement of `const` helps in writing more robust code and avoiding unintended side effects, especially in APIs and libraries.

Interview Question 67: Can You Increment a Pointer to an Array?

Why This Question Is Asked:

Pointer arithmetic is a fundamental concept in C. Interviewers ask this to evaluate your understanding of how pointers work with arrays and how memory is accessed.

What the Interviewer Wants to Know:

- Do you understand pointer arithmetic?
- Can you explain how pointers interact with arrays?
- Are you aware of how increments affect the pointer's position?

How to Structure Your Answer:

1. Clarify that pointers can be incremented
2. Show how this works with arrays
3. Provide a code example

Sample Answer (Beginner):

"Yes, you can increment a pointer to an array. It moves to the next element in the array."

Sample Answer (Experienced):

"Yes, in C you can increment a pointer to an array. When you increment a pointer, it moves to the next element of the type it points to:

```
int arr[] = {10, 20, 30};
int *ptr = arr;
ptr++; // now points to arr[1]
```

This works because ptr++ increases the pointer by sizeof(int) (or the size of the element it points to). You can use this to iterate through arrays efficiently.

Note: You cannot increment the array name itself (e.g., arr++ is illegal), because array names are not modifiable lvalues."

Beginner Tip:

Use pointer increment in loops with caution to avoid accessing memory out of bounds.

Final Thought:

Pointer arithmetic is powerful and efficient. It enables fast traversal through arrays but must be used carefully to ensure memory safety.

Interview Question 68: What Happens When You Dereference a NULL Pointer?

Why This Question Is Asked:

Dereferencing a NULL pointer is a critical error in C programming. Interviewers ask this to evaluate your understanding of pointer safety and runtime behavior.

What the Interviewer Wants to Know:

- Do you understand the concept of a NULL pointer?
- Do you know what dereferencing means?
- Are you aware of the consequences and how to prevent such errors?

How to Structure Your Answer:
1. Define what it means to dereference a pointer
2. Explain what a NULL pointer is
3. Describe what happens when you dereference a NULL pointer

Sample Answer (Beginner):
"If you try to dereference a NULL pointer, the program will crash. It's like trying to access memory that doesn't exist."

Sample Answer (Experienced):

"Dereferencing a pointer means accessing the value at the memory address the pointer holds. A NULL pointer points to no valid memory location. So, dereferencing it results in undefined behavior — typically a segmentation fault or crash:

```
int *ptr = NULL;
*ptr = 10; // crash or segmentation fault
```

Operating systems protect NULL (address 0) to catch such errors. It's a common runtime bug in C. To avoid it:

- Always check if the pointer is NULL before dereferencing:

```
if (ptr != NULL) {
    *ptr = 10;
}
```

- Use defensive programming techniques and tools like Valgrind."

Beginner Tip:

Always initialize your pointers and check for NULL before using them.

Final Thought:

Dereferencing a NULL pointer is a serious error. It leads to crashes and hard-to-debug issues, especially in larger codebases. Defensive coding is essential to avoid this mistake.

Interview Question 69: What Is a Segmentation Fault?

Why This Question Is Asked:

Segmentation faults are common runtime errors in C. Interviewers ask this to evaluate your understanding of memory access violations and how to avoid them.

What the Interviewer Wants to Know:

- Do you know what causes a segmentation fault?
- Can you identify common situations where they occur?
- Do you understand how to prevent or debug them?

How to Structure Your Answer:

1. Define what a segmentation fault is
2. Explain how and why it happens
3. Provide examples and mention tools to diagnose

Sample Answer (Beginner):

"A segmentation fault happens when a program tries to access memory that it doesn't have permission to use."

Sample Answer (Experienced):

"A segmentation fault (often called segfault) occurs when a program attempts to read from or write to a restricted area of memory. Common causes include:

- Dereferencing a NULL or uninitialized pointer
- Accessing memory beyond array bounds
- Writing to read-only memory (e.g., string literals)
- Using dangling or freed pointers

Example:

```
int *ptr = NULL;
*ptr = 5; // segmentation fault
```
The operating system stops the program to protect memory integrity. To prevent it:
- Initialize pointers properly
- Use bounds checking on arrays
- Use tools like Valgrind or AddressSanitizer for debugging"

Beginner Tip:

Never dereference a pointer unless you're sure it points to valid, allocated memory.

Final Thought:

Segmentation faults signal serious memory errors. Preventing them requires careful memory handling and thorough testing.

Interview Question 70: What Is Pointer Decay?

Why This Question Is Asked:

Pointer decay is a subtle yet crucial concept in C, especially when working with arrays and functions. Interviewers ask this to test your deeper understanding of how arrays behave when passed to functions.

What the Interviewer Wants to Know:

- Do you understand how arrays and pointers are related?
- Can you explain what happens when an array is passed to a function?
- Are you aware of how this affects array size and pointer arithmetic?

How to Structure Your Answer:

1. Define what pointer decay is
2. Describe when and how it occurs
3. Provide examples and implications

Sample Answer (Beginner):

"Pointer decay means that an array turns into a pointer to its first element when passed to a function."

Sample Answer (Experienced):

"Pointer decay refers to the process where an array name is automatically converted to a pointer to its first element in most expressions, particularly when passed to a function. For example:

```
void printArray(int arr[]) {
    // arr is actually treated as int *arr
}
```

This means:

- The size of the array cannot be determined inside the function using `sizeof(arr)`
- You can still access elements using pointer arithmetic: `*(arr + i)`

Pointer decay occurs:

- When arrays are passed to functions
- In most expressions, except `sizeof`, &, and string literals

Beginner Tip:

To preserve the size of an array in functions, pass it along with its size explicitly.

Final Thought:

Pointer decay is fundamental for understanding how arrays work in C. Awareness of this behavior helps you avoid bugs and write safer, more efficient code.

Interview Question 71: How Do You Create an Array of Pointers?

Why This Question Is Asked:

Arrays of pointers are useful in dynamic data management, especially for handling strings or arrays of varying sizes. Interviewers ask this to test your understanding of pointers, arrays, and memory organization.

What the Interviewer Wants to Know:

- Can you declare and initialize an array of pointers?
- Do you know when to use arrays of pointers vs. multidimensional arrays?
- Can you provide examples and explain how to access elements?

How to Structure Your Answer:

1. Define what an array of pointers is
2. Explain how to declare and use it
3. Provide a code example

Sample Answer (Beginner):

"An array of pointers is a collection of pointer variables stored in an array. Each pointer can point to a different data item."

Sample Answer (Experienced):

"An array of pointers in C is declared as:

```
int *arr[5]; // array of 5 int pointers
```

Each element in the array is a pointer that can point to a separate integer:

```
int a = 10, b = 20;
arr[0] = &a;
arr[1] = &b;
```

This is useful when you need to reference different memory blocks, such as strings:

```c
char *names[] = {"Alice", "Bob", "Charlie"};
printf("%s\n", names[1]); // prints "Bob"
```

Beginner Tip:

Always ensure that each pointer in the array is initialized before dereferencing.

Final Thought:

Arrays of pointers offer flexibility in accessing variable-length or dynamically allocated data. Mastering this concept is key for efficient memory management in C.

Interview Question 72: How Are Pointers Used in Linked Lists?

Why This Question Is Asked:

Linked lists are a fundamental data structure in C, and understanding how pointers enable their structure is crucial. Interviewers ask this to assess your grasp of dynamic data structures and pointer manipulation.

What the Interviewer Wants to Know:

- Do you understand how pointers connect elements in a linked list?
- Can you explain how to create, traverse, and manipulate a linked list using pointers?
- Are you comfortable with dynamic memory and struct usage?

How to Structure Your Answer:
1. Define what a linked list is
2. Describe how pointers link nodes together
3. Provide a basic example of a node and operations

Sample Answer (Beginner):

"In a linked list, each node contains data and a pointer to the next node. Pointers are used to connect these nodes into a chain."

Sample Answer (Experienced):

"Pointers are essential in linked lists because each node must store a reference to the next node. A typical node is defined like this:

```
struct Node {
    int data;
    struct Node *next;
};
```

To create and link nodes:

```
struct Node *head = malloc(sizeof(struct Node));
head->data = 1;
head->next = malloc(sizeof(struct Node));
head->next->data = 2;
head->next->next = NULL;
```

Here, next is a pointer that connects one node to another, forming a chain. You use these pointers to insert, delete, and traverse the list."

Beginner Tip:

Always allocate memory for new nodes and check if the pointer is NULL after malloc().

Final Thought:

Pointers make linked lists dynamic and flexible, unlike arrays. Mastering them is key to implementing stacks, queues, and other advanced structures in C.

Interview Question 73: What Is the Use of void * Pointer?

Why This Question Is Asked:

The void * pointer is a versatile feature in C. Interviewers ask this to test your understanding of generic pointers and how C handles type-agnostic memory access.

What the Interviewer Wants to Know:

- Can you define a void * pointer and its purpose?
- Do you know how to cast and use it safely?
- Are you aware of common use cases in APIs and libraries?

How to Structure Your Answer:

1. Define what a void * pointer is
2. Explain how it's used in a type-independent way
3. Provide examples and mention when to cast it

Sample Answer (Beginner):

"A void * pointer is a generic pointer that can point to any data type, but it cannot be dereferenced directly."

Sample Answer (Experienced):

"A void * pointer in C is a generic pointer that can hold the address of any data type:

```
void *ptr;
int x = 10;
ptr = &x;
```

Since it has no type, you must cast it before dereferencing:

```
printf("%d\n", *(int *)ptr);
```

Use cases include:

- Writing generic functions (like `qsort()` or `memcpy()`)
- Abstracting data structures
- Working with dynamically allocated memory

Limitations:

- Cannot perform pointer arithmetic
- Must be cast to the correct type before use

Beginner Tip:

Always cast a `void *` to the proper type before dereferencing to avoid errors or undefined behavior.

Final Thought:

The `void *` pointer makes C flexible for low-level and generic programming. Used wisely, it enables reusable and abstracted code.

Interview Question 74: What Is Memory Alignment?

Why This Question Is Asked:

Memory alignment affects performance, data access, and portability in C programs. Interviewers ask this to evaluate your low-level understanding of how data is stored and accessed in memory.

What the Interviewer Wants to Know:

- Can you define memory alignment?
- Do you understand how the CPU and memory interact?
- Are you aware of structure padding and alignment requirements?

How to Structure Your Answer:

1. Define memory alignment
2. Explain why it's needed
3. Provide examples, especially in the context of structs

Sample Answer (Beginner):

"Memory alignment means placing data at memory addresses that are multiples of word size, so the CPU can access it efficiently."

Sample Answer (Experienced):

"Memory alignment refers to arranging variables in memory at addresses that match their size requirements for optimal access. For instance, a 4-byte `int` is typically aligned to a 4-byte boundary.

This ensures:

- Faster memory access (due to how CPUs fetch data)
- Avoidance of hardware exceptions on some architectures

Example (struct padding):

```
struct A {
    char c;
    int i;
};
```

Here, padding bytes may be added after `char` to align `int` to a 4-byte boundary. Misalignment can lead to performance penalties or crashes on strict architectures.

Beginner Tip:

Use `sizeof()` to check structure size, and `#pragma pack` or `__attribute__((packed))` to control alignment if necessary.

Final Thought:

Memory alignment is crucial for efficient and portable code. Awareness of alignment issues helps avoid subtle bugs and optimize performance on embedded and low-level systems.

Interview Question 75: What Is Pointer Aliasing?

Why This Question Is Asked:

Pointer aliasing can lead to subtle bugs and performance issues in C. Interviewers ask this to test your understanding of how multiple pointers might refer to the same memory and how it affects optimization and behavior.

What the Interviewer Wants to Know:

- Do you understand what pointer aliasing means?
- Can you explain how it happens and its implications?
- Are you aware of how compilers treat aliasing in optimization?

How to Structure Your Answer:

1. Define pointer aliasing
2. Explain how it can affect behavior and performance
3. Provide examples and mention the `restrict` keyword

Sample Answer (Beginner):

"Pointer aliasing happens when two or more pointers refer to the same memory location. Changing one affects the others."

Sample Answer (Experienced):

"Pointer aliasing occurs when multiple pointers reference the same memory location. For example:

```
int x = 10;
int *p1 = &x;
int *p2 = &x;
```

Here, p1 and p2 alias the same variable x. Changes via one pointer are visible through the other.

Aliasing can:

- Make programs harder to understand and debug
- Inhibit compiler optimizations, as the compiler must assume memory could change via any pointer

To help compilers, C99 introduced the `restrict` keyword, which tells the compiler that only one pointer will access a memory location:

```
void process(int *restrict a, int *restrict b);
```

This allows for more aggressive optimizations.

Beginner Tip:

Be cautious when passing multiple pointers to the same function. Document whether they can alias.

Final Thought:

Understanding pointer aliasing is crucial for writing safe, predictable, and optimized C code. It's especially important in performance-critical or parallel applications.

Section 4: Structures, Unions & Preprocessors (76–90)

Interview Question 76: What Is a Structure in C?

Why This Question Is Asked:

Structures are fundamental for organizing related data in C. Interviewers ask this to assess your understanding of how to define and use complex data types.

What the Interviewer Wants to Know:

- Can you define and use a structure?
- Do you understand how to access structure members?
- Can you explain the difference between structures and arrays?

How to Structure Your Answer:

1. Define what a structure is
2. Explain how it is declared and used
3. Provide an example with member access

Sample Answer (Beginner):

"A structure is a user-defined data type that groups variables of different types under a single name."

Sample Answer (Experienced):

"In C, a structure is a composite data type that allows grouping variables of different types together. It is useful for modeling real-world entities:

```
struct Person {
    char name[50];
    int age;
    float height;
};
```

```
struct Person p1 = {"Alice", 30, 5.5};
printf("%s is %d years old.\n", p1.name, p1.age);
```

You can access members using the dot operator (.), or arrow operator (->) if you have a pointer to a structure.

Structures allow organizing data logically and are foundational in building linked lists, trees, and complex applications."

Beginner Tip:

Use . to access members with variables and -> with pointers.

Final Thought:

Structures bring clarity and flexibility to C programs by bundling related data. They are essential for organizing and managing real-world data in code.

Interview Question 77: How Do You Declare and Use Structures?

Why This Question Is Asked:

Declaring and using structures is key to organizing complex data in C. Interviewers ask this to assess your ability to define structured types and work with their instances.

What the Interviewer Wants to Know:
- Do you understand the syntax of declaring a structure?
- Can you create and use structure variables?
- Do you know how to access and modify structure members?

How to Structure Your Answer:
1. Explain the structure declaration syntax
2. Show how to create structure variables
3. Demonstrate accessing and modifying members

Sample Answer (Beginner):

"To declare a structure, I use the `struct` keyword with a block of member variables. I can then define variables using the structure name."

Sample Answer (Experienced):

"In C, you declare a structure using the `struct` keyword followed by a definition:

```
struct Point {
    int x;
    int y;
};
```

To use it, create a variable of the structure type:

```
struct Point p1;
p1.x = 10;
p1.y = 20;
```

To use a pointer to a structure:

```
struct Point *ptr = &p1;
printf("%d %d\n", ptr->x, ptr->y);
```

This enables structured representation of data and is essential in data modeling."

Beginner Tip:

Remember to use . for regular variables and -> for pointers to access structure members.

Final Thought:

Structures are foundational in C for managing related data efficiently. Mastering their usage helps in building robust and organized code.

Interview Question 78: How Do You Pass Structures to Functions?

Why This Question Is Asked:

Passing structures to functions is a common practice for modular programming. Interviewers ask this to assess your knowledge of memory handling, function design, and efficiency in C.

What the Interviewer Wants to Know:

- Do you know how to pass structures by value and by reference?
- Can you explain the implications of each method?
- Are you aware of how structure size affects function calls?

How to Structure Your Answer:

1. Describe the two main ways to pass structures
2. Provide syntax and examples for both
3. Explain when to use each method

Sample Answer (Beginner):

"You can pass a structure to a function either directly (by value) or using a pointer (by reference)."

Sample Answer (Experienced):

"In C, structures can be passed to functions in two ways:

- **By Value:**

```
void display(struct Point p) {
    printf("%d %d\n", p.x, p.y);
}
```

This creates a copy of the structure. Changes made in the function don't affect the original.

```
void update(struct Point *p) {
    p->x = 10;
    p->y = 20;
}
```

This allows modifying the original structure.

Use by value for small, read-only structures. **Use by reference** for large structures or when modification is needed."

Beginner Tip:

Use -> to access members when using pointers to structures.

Final Thought:

Choosing between value and reference impacts performance and behavior. Understanding both is key to writing efficient and predictable C functions.

Interview Question 79: What Is the Difference Between Structure and Union?

Why This Question Is Asked:

Understanding the difference between structures and unions is key to efficient memory use in C. Interviewers ask this to evaluate your knowledge of memory allocation and data organization.

What the Interviewer Wants to Know:

- Do you understand how structures and unions store data?
- Can you explain the memory implications?
- Can you describe when to use each?

How to Structure Your Answer:

1. Define structures and unions
2. Compare their memory allocation
3. Provide use cases and examples

Sample Answer (Beginner):

"In a structure, all members have their own memory. In a union, all members share the same memory space."

Sample Answer (Experienced):

"Structures and unions are both user-defined data types in C, but they differ in memory handling:

- **Structure (struct):**
  - Allocates separate memory for each member.
  - Size = sum of all members (plus padding).
  - All members can be accessed independently.

```
struct Example {
    int a;
    float b;
};
```

- **Union (union):**
  - All members share the same memory.
  - Size = size of the largest member.
  - Only one member holds a valid value at a time.

```
union Example {
    int a;
    float b;
};
```

Use structures when you need to store multiple independent values. **Use unions** when only one value is needed at a time to save memory (e.g., variant data types).

Beginner Tip:

Accessing a different member of a union than the one most recently written can lead to undefined behavior.

Final Thought:

Choose structures for full data access and unions for memory-efficient design when only one member is active at a time.

Interview Question 80: What Is a `typedef`?

Why This Question Is Asked:

The `typedef` keyword enhances code readability and maintainability. Interviewers ask this to test your ability to abstract complex data types and create custom type names.

What the Interviewer Wants to Know:

- Do you understand what `typedef` does in C?
- Can you explain how it simplifies code?
- Are you able to use `typedef` with structures and pointers?

How to Structure Your Answer:

1. Define what `typedef` is and its purpose
2. Show how to declare and use `typedef`
3. Provide common examples, especially with structs

Sample Answer (Beginner):

"`typedef` is used to create a new name for an existing data type, making the code easier to read."

Sample Answer (Experienced):

"In C, typedef allows you to define a new name (alias) for an existing type. It's commonly used to simplify long declarations:

```
typedef unsigned int uint;
uint a = 5;
```

It's also used with structures:

```
typedef struct {
    int x;
    int y;
} Point;
```

```
Point p1 = {10, 20};
```

This removes the need to use struct keyword every time.

Benefits:

- Simplifies complex declarations
- Improves code readability
- Useful for portability and API design

Beginner Tip:

Use typedef to shorten repetitive type definitions, especially for structures and pointers.

Final Thought:

typedef is a powerful tool for abstraction and cleaner code. It's widely used in headers, libraries, and large-scale applications.

Interview Question 81: What Are Nested Structures?

Why This Question Is Asked:

Nested structures help organize complex data models. Interviewers ask this to test your understanding of advanced structure usage and data grouping in C.

What the Interviewer Wants to Know:

- Can you define and use a structure inside another structure?
- Do you understand the syntax and how to access nested members?
- Can you explain when nested structures are useful?

How to Structure Your Answer:

1. Define what a nested structure is
2. Explain how to declare and use them
3. Provide an example

Sample Answer (Beginner):

"A nested structure is a structure defined inside another structure. It helps group related data hierarchically."

Sample Answer (Experienced):

"In C, a nested structure means having one structure as a member of another structure. This is useful for grouping related subcomponents:

```
struct Date {
    int day, month, year;
};

struct Employee {
    char name[50];
    struct Date joiningDate;  // nested structure
```

```
};

struct Employee e1;
e1.joiningDate.day = 1;
e1.joiningDate.month = 1;
e1.joiningDate.year = 2020;
```

You access members using the dot operator multiple times. Nested structures simplify organization of complex data."

Beginner Tip:

Use nested structures when a part of your data logically groups into its own structure.

Final Thought:

Nested structures promote clarity and modularity in code. They are a good design choice for managing complex entities with sub-components.

Interview Question 82: How Is Memory Allocated for Structures?

Why This Question Is Asked:

Understanding memory allocation for structures is important for performance, alignment, and system-level programming. Interviewers ask this to test your knowledge of how memory is laid out in C.

What the Interviewer Wants to Know:

- Do you understand how memory is allocated for structure members?
- Can you explain padding and alignment?
- Are you aware of how to inspect and optimize structure size?

How to Structure Your Answer:

1. Describe how memory is allocated for each member
2. Explain the role of padding and alignment
3. Provide example and use `sizeof()` to show effects

Sample Answer (Beginner):

"Memory for a structure is allocated as a block that includes space for all members, plus padding to align members properly."

Sample Answer (Experienced):

"When a structure is declared, memory is allocated sequentially for its members. However, compilers may add padding to ensure proper alignment based on data type size. For example:

```
struct Example {
    char a;     // 1 byte
    int b;      // 4 bytes (requires alignment)
};
```

Here, 3 bytes of padding are added after `char` a so that `int` b aligns on a 4-byte boundary. Total size becomes 8 bytes instead of 5.

You can check this with:

```
printf("%lu\n", sizeof(struct Example));
```

To reduce size, reorder members by decreasing size or use compiler-specific pragmas to pack structures.

Beginner Tip:
Use `sizeof()` to check structure size and be aware of padding when designing memory-efficient code.

Final Thought:
Knowing how memory is allocated for structures helps you write efficient and portable programs. It's especially important in embedded and low-level systems.

Interview Question 83: What Is a Bit Field in Structures?

Why This Question Is Asked:

Bit fields are useful for memory-efficient data representation. Interviewers ask this to assess your knowledge of low-level memory usage and custom-sized data members in C.

What the Interviewer Wants to Know:

- Do you understand what a bit field is?
- Can you declare and use bit fields in structures?
- Are you aware of their limitations and benefits?

How to Structure Your Answer:

1. Define a bit field in the context of structures
2. Explain how and why they are used
3. Provide a code example

Sample Answer (Beginner):

"A bit field allows you to allocate a specific number of bits to a structure member, which helps save memory."

Sample Answer (Experienced):

"Bit fields in C are used within structures to allocate a precise number of bits to a variable. This is useful in situations where memory is limited or when mapping hardware registers.

Example:

```
struct Flags {
    unsigned int flag1 : 1;
    unsigned int flag2 : 1;
    unsigned int mode  : 2;
};
```

This defines a structure where `flag1` and `flag2` use 1 bit each, and `mode` uses 2 bits. The total memory used may be less than using full `int` variables.

Use Cases:

- Hardware programming
- Protocol design
- Compact data storage

Limitations:

- Bit fields cannot be referenced with pointers
- Implementation-defined behavior across compilers

Beginner Tip:

Use bit fields only when you need fine-grained control over memory layout or size.

Final Thought:

Bit fields are a powerful tool for optimizing memory and interfacing with hardware. However, they should be used carefully due to potential portability issues.

Interview Question 84: What Is the Use of Union?

Why This Question Is Asked:

Unions are useful for memory optimization and type-flexible data structures. Interviewers ask this to test your understanding of union behavior and practical use cases in C programming.

What the Interviewer Wants to Know:

- Do you understand how unions work?
- Can you explain situations where using a union is better than a structure?
- Are you aware of limitations and precautions?

How to Structure Your Answer:

1. Define what a union is
2. Explain how it works and differs from a structure
3. Provide examples and typical use cases

Sample Answer (Beginner):

"A union is a data type where all members share the same memory location. It is used when only one of the members is needed at a time."

Sample Answer (Experienced):

"A union in C is a user-defined data type where all members share the same memory location. This means only one member holds a valid value at any given time. It is declared similarly to a structure:

```
union Data {
    int i;
    float f;
    char str[20];
};
```

All members share memory, and the size of the union equals the size of its largest member.

Use Cases:

- Efficient memory usage when only one member is active at a time
- Implementing variant data types (like in compilers or protocols)
- Representing hardware registers

Caution:

- Accessing inactive members leads to undefined behavior

Beginner Tip:

Always track which union member is currently in use to avoid bugs.

Final Thought:

Unions are powerful for saving space and implementing type-flexible data. When used correctly, they contribute to efficient and elegant low-level programming.

Interview Question 85: What Is the Difference Between #define and const?

Why This Question Is Asked:

Both #define and const are used to define constants in C, but they differ significantly in behavior and usage. Interviewers ask this to test your understanding of preprocessor directives and constant variables.

What the Interviewer Wants to Know:

- Do you understand the difference in how #define and const are handled?
- Can you explain when to use each appropriately?
- Are you aware of their scope, type safety, and debugging implications?

How to Structure Your Answer:

1. Define both #define and const
2. Compare their behaviors and use cases
3. Provide examples

Sample Answer (Beginner):

"`#define` is a preprocessor directive that replaces code before compilation. `const` is a keyword that makes a variable read-only."

Sample Answer (Experienced):

"`#define` creates a macro, which is replaced by the preprocessor before compilation:

```
#define PI 3.14
```

It has no type and can cause debugging difficulties. `const` declares a typed constant:

```
const float pi = 3.14;
```

Key Differences:

- `#define` is a textual substitution; `const` is a typed variable
- `#define` has no scope; `const` respects C's scope rules
- `const` allows for better debugging and type checking

When to Use:

- Use `const` when type safety and debugging are important
- Use `#define` for conditional compilation or header guards

Beginner Tip:

Prefer `const` for defining constants in modern C programming. It's safer and easier to debug.

Final Thought:

Choosing between `#define` and `const` affects code clarity, safety, and maintainability. `const` is generally preferred unless macro behavior is explicitly needed.

Interview Question 86: What Is a Macro?

Why This Question Is Asked:

Macros are widely used in C for code reuse, conditional compilation, and performance optimization. Interviewers ask this to test your understanding of the preprocessor and compile-time code manipulation.

What the Interviewer Wants to Know:

- Can you define what a macro is in C?
- Do you understand how macros are expanded by the preprocessor?
- Are you aware of different types of macros and their limitations?

How to Structure Your Answer:

1. Define what a macro is
2. Explain how macros are used and processed
3. Provide examples, including parameterized macros

Sample Answer (Beginner):

"A macro is a fragment of code that is given a name using #define. The preprocessor replaces it before compilation."

Sample Answer (Experienced):

"A macro in C is defined using the #define directive. It performs text substitution during preprocessing, before actual compilation. Example:

#define PI 3.14159

You can also define parameterized macros:

#define SQUARE(x) ((x)*(x))

Macros are fast because they avoid function call overhead. However, they:

- Lack type safety
- Can cause unexpected bugs if not parenthesized properly

Macros are also used for:

- Header guards
- Conditional compilation (`#ifdef`, `#ifndef`)

Beginner Tip:

Always use parentheses in macro definitions to avoid precedence issues.

Final Thought:

Macros are a powerful preprocessor feature in C, but they must be used with caution. For type safety and debugging, prefer `const` or `inline` functions where applicable.

Interview Question 87: What Are Predefined Macros?

Why This Question Is Asked:

Predefined macros offer compile-time information like file name, date, or line number. Interviewers ask this to assess your familiarity with C's preprocessor and how to leverage it for debugging or conditional logic.

What the Interviewer Wants to Know:

- Do you know what predefined macros are in C?
- Can you list and explain common predefined macros?
- Do you understand how and when to use them?

How to Structure Your Answer:

1. Define what predefined macros are
2. List common predefined macros and their purposes
3. Provide usage examples

Sample Answer (Beginner):

"Predefined macros are built-in macros provided by the compiler that contain useful information about the file, date, or time."

Sample Answer (Experienced):

"Predefined macros in C are built-in identifiers provided by the compiler that give contextual information during preprocessing. Common predefined macros include:

- __FILE__ – current filename
- __LINE__ – current line number
- __DATE__ – compilation date
- __TIME__ – compilation time
- __STDC__ – defined if the compiler conforms to the ANSI C standard

Example:

```
printf("Compiled on %s at %s in file %s at line %d\n",
__DATE__, __TIME__, __FILE__, __LINE__);
```

These macros are useful for logging, debugging, and conditional compilation.

Beginner Tip:

Use these macros in debugging statements to trace issues without manual logging.

Final Thought:

Predefined macros are simple yet powerful tools for providing contextual info and improving the maintainability of your C programs.

Interview Question 88: What Is Conditional Compilation?

Why This Question Is Asked:

Conditional compilation allows different parts of code to be compiled based on defined macros or platform-specific settings. Interviewers ask this to test your knowledge of the C preprocessor and portability techniques.

What the Interviewer Wants to Know:

- Do you understand what conditional compilation is?
- Can you use preprocessor directives like `#ifdef`, `#ifndef`, and `#if`?
- Are you aware of its usefulness in cross-platform or debug builds?

How to Structure Your Answer:

1. Define conditional compilation
2. Explain common directives used
3. Provide examples and use cases

Sample Answer (Beginner):

"Conditional compilation means compiling certain parts of code based on conditions, usually defined with macros."

Sample Answer (Experienced):

"Conditional compilation in C uses preprocessor directives to include or exclude code during compilation, depending on the conditions. Common directives:

- `#ifdef MACRO` – checks if MACRO is defined
- `#ifndef MACRO` – checks if MACRO is not defined
- `#if, #else, #elif, #endif` – standard conditionals

Example:

```
#define DEBUG

#ifdef DEBUG
    printf("Debug mode\n");
#endif
```

This allows:

- Debug vs. release builds
- Platform-specific code blocks
- Optional features based on configuration

Beginner Tip:

Use header guards (#ifndef, #define, #endif) to avoid multiple inclusions.

Final Thought:

Conditional compilation provides flexibility and maintainability in C programs, especially in large, portable codebases.

Interview Question 89: What Is the Difference Between #include <...> and #include "..."?

Why This Question Is Asked:
This question evaluates your understanding of how the preprocessor handles file inclusion, which is crucial for managing dependencies in C projects.

What the Interviewer Wants to Know:
- Do you understand the file search order used by the compiler?
- Can you explain when to use angle brackets vs. double quotes?
- Are you aware of typical use cases for system vs. user-defined headers?

How to Structure Your Answer:

1. Describe the syntax and purpose of each inclusion style
2. Explain the search behavior
3. Provide best practices

Sample Answer (Beginner):

"`#include <...>` is for system headers, and `#include "..."` is for user-defined headers."

Sample Answer (Experienced):

"In C, `#include <...>` and `#include "..."` are both used to include header files, but they differ in how the preprocessor searches for the file:

- `#include <file>`: Tells the preprocessor to search for the file in the standard system directories. It is typically used for standard library headers like:

`#include <stdio.h>`

- `#include "file"`: Tells the preprocessor to search the current directory (or user-specified directories) first, and then system directories. It is used for user-defined headers:

`#include "myheader.h"`

Best Practices:
- Use `<...>` for standard or library headers
- Use `"..."` for your own or local project files

Beginner Tip:
Mixing them can lead to errors if the file isn't found. Always be clear about the file's location.

Final Thought:
Understanding `#include` behavior is essential for managing header files, avoiding conflicts, and ensuring portable, maintainable C code.

Interview Question 90: What Is the Use of #pragma Directive?

Why This Question Is Asked:

The #pragma directive gives compiler-specific instructions and affects code compilation. Interviewers ask this to test your awareness of advanced compiler features and portability considerations.

What the Interviewer Wants to Know:

- Do you know what #pragma does?
- Can you provide examples of commonly used #pragma directives?
- Are you aware that #pragma is compiler-specific?

How to Structure Your Answer:

1. Define what the #pragma directive is
2. Describe how it is used and its flexibility
3. Provide examples with common use cases

Sample Answer (Beginner):

"The #pragma directive is used to give special instructions to the compiler. It's often used for optimizations or controlling warnings."

Sample Answer (Experienced):

"#pragma is a preprocessor directive that allows the programmer to enable or disable specific features of the compiler. It is compiler-dependent and used for:

- Disabling warnings
- Aligning structures
- Packing structures to avoid padding

Example:

```
#pragma pack(1)
struct MyStruct {
    char a;
    int b;
};
#pragma pack()
```

This tells the compiler to pack the structure with 1-byte alignment, minimizing padding.

Another example disables a specific warning (MSVC):

```
#pragma warning(disable : 4996)
```

Beginner Tip:

Always check documentation for your specific compiler when using #pragma, as it may not be portable.

Final Thought:

#pragma is a powerful tool for fine-tuning compilation behavior but should be used judiciously due to portability concerns.

Section 5: Advanced & Practical Scenarios (91–101)

Interview Question 91: How Is C Used in Embedded Systems?

Why This Question Is Asked:

C is the dominant language for embedded programming. Interviewers ask this to test your understanding of system-level programming, hardware interaction, and the efficiency benefits of using C in embedded applications.

What the Interviewer Wants to Know:

- Do you understand why C is preferred for embedded systems?
- Can you explain how C interacts with hardware?
- Are you aware of C's role in memory and performance-sensitive environments?

How to Structure Your Answer:

1. Explain what embedded systems are
2. Describe why C is suitable for them
3. Provide examples of how C is used in real-world embedded applications

Sample Answer (Beginner):

"C is used in embedded systems because it provides low-level access to memory and hardware while being easier to write than assembly language."

Sample Answer (Experienced):

"C is the most widely used language for embedded systems because it offers a good balance between control and abstraction. Key reasons include:

- **Direct hardware access**: C supports pointers and bit manipulation, allowing control of memory-mapped I/O and registers.
- **Efficient use of resources**: It compiles to highly optimized machine code suitable for devices with limited CPU and memory.
- **Portability**: Code can be reused across different microcontrollers with minimal changes.
- **Real-time performance**: C allows writing deterministic, time-critical routines often required in embedded systems.

Example:

```
#define LED_PORT (*(volatile unsigned char*)0x20)
void turnOnLED() {
    LED_PORT |= 0x01; // Set bit to turn on LED
}
```

This example shows how C can manipulate a hardware register directly.

Use Cases:

- Firmware for microcontrollers
- Real-time control systems
- Consumer electronics, automotive systems, IoT devices

Beginner Tip:

Learn to read and write hardware registers and use embedded development tools like debuggers and in-circuit emulators.

Final Thought:

C's performance, portability, and close-to-hardware capabilities make it ideal for embedded system development, from industrial control to consumer electronics.

Interview Question 92: How Do You Debug a C Program?

Why This Question Is Asked:

Debugging is an essential skill for any C programmer. Interviewers ask this to assess your approach to identifying and resolving bugs in C code using tools and techniques.

What the Interviewer Wants to Know:

- Do you know how to find and fix errors in a C program?
- Can you use debugging tools effectively?
- Are you aware of best practices in debugging?

How to Structure Your Answer:

1. Explain the typical steps in debugging
2. List common tools and techniques
3. Share tips and strategies to prevent or trace issues

Sample Answer (Beginner):

"To debug a C program, I look for logical or runtime errors, add print statements, and recompile the program to see what goes wrong."

Sample Answer (Experienced):

"To debug a C program efficiently, I follow a systematic approach:

1. **Reproduce the Bug**: Identify the exact input or scenario where the issue appears.
2. **Use Print Statements**: Temporarily insert `printf()` to trace variable values and execution flow.
3. **Use a Debugger**: I use gdb (GNU Debugger) to set breakpoints, step through code, inspect variables, and understand the call stack.

```
gcc -g program.c -o program
./gdb program
gdb> break main
gdb> run
gdb> next / print var_name
```

4. **Check Compiler Warnings**: Always compile with `-Wall` to catch
   potential issues.
5. **Static Analyzers**: Tools like `cppcheck` or `clang-tidy` help
   detect bugs without running the program.
6. **Valgrind**: For memory issues, I use Valgrind to catch leaks and
   invalid memory accesses:

```
valgrind ./program
```

Beginner Tip:

Never ignore compiler warnings—they often point to bugs before they
crash.

Final Thought:

Efficient debugging combines systematic problem-solving with the right
tools. Mastering debugging is essential to becoming a reliable and
productive C programmer.

Interview Question 93: What Are Common Runtime Errors in C?

Why This Question Is Asked:

Runtime errors can lead to unpredictable behavior and crashes.
Interviewers ask this to evaluate your understanding of error types and
your ability to diagnose and prevent them.

What the Interviewer Wants to Know:

- Can you identify different kinds of runtime errors in C?
- Do you know how to prevent or handle them?
- Are you familiar with the tools used to detect such errors?

How to Structure Your Answer:

1. Define what runtime errors are
2. List common types of runtime errors
3. Provide examples and prevention techniques

Sample Answer (Beginner):

"Runtime errors are bugs that occur when the program is running. They often crash the program or cause it to behave incorrectly."

Sample Answer (Experienced):

"Runtime errors in C are errors that occur while the program is executing. Common runtime errors include:

1. **Segmentation Faults** – Occur when accessing invalid memory, such as dereferencing NULL or out-of-bounds pointers.
2. **Division by Zero** – Causes undefined behavior and usually crashes the program.
3. **Buffer Overflows** – Writing beyond the bounds of an array, corrupting memory.
4. **Memory Leaks** – Allocating memory and never freeing it, leading to increased memory usage.
5. **Dangling Pointers** – Using pointers after memory has been freed.
6. **Uninitialized Variables** – Reading values before they're assigned, leading to unpredictable behavior.
7. **File Handling Errors** – Not checking if a file opened successfully before reading/writing.

Prevention Tips:

- Use tools like Valgrind, AddressSanitizer
- Enable compiler warnings (`-Wall`, `-Wextra`)
- Initialize all variables
- Validate user input
- Always check return values from functions (like `malloc()` or `fopen()`)

Beginner Tip:

Run your code through a memory checker to catch errors before they crash your app.

Final Thought:

C gives you great control over memory, but that power comes with risk. Knowing the common runtime errors and how to prevent them is crucial for stable software.

Interview Question 94: How Do You Handle Errors in C?

Why This Question Is Asked:

Error handling is essential for writing robust and user-friendly programs. Interviewers ask this to evaluate your ability to detect and respond to errors in a structured and predictable way.

What the Interviewer Wants to Know:

- Are you familiar with techniques for detecting and reporting errors?
- Do you understand standard error-handling practices in C?
- Can you implement safe and maintainable error-handling logic?

How to Structure Your Answer:

1. Explain the different ways C supports error handling
2. Provide examples using return values, `errno`, and `perror()`
3. Share tips for effective error management

Sample Answer (Beginner):

"In C, I usually check return values from functions and print an error message if something goes wrong."

Sample Answer (Experienced):

"In C, error handling is typically done using return values and standard error indicators. Some common methods include:

1. **Return Codes**: Most functions return a value that indicates success (usually 0) or failure (non-zero or NULL).

```
FILE *fp = fopen("file.txt", "r");
if (fp == NULL) {
    perror("Error opening file");
    return 1;
}
```

2. **errno and perror() / strerror()**: The global variable `errno` provides error codes. `perror()` prints a human-readable error message.

```
#include <errno.h>
#include <string.h>

if (malloc(0) == NULL) {
    fprintf(stderr, "Memory error: %s\n",
strerror(errno));
}
```

3. **assert()**: Used for debugging, it terminates the program if an expression evaluates to false.

```
#include <assert.h>
assert(ptr != NULL);
```

4. **Custom error-handling functions**: For large projects, I implement centralized logging or error-handling routines.

Beginner Tip:

Always check return values of system calls and standard library functions—assume nothing will always succeed.

Final Thought:

In C, error handling requires discipline and consistency. Using return values, errno, and debug tools effectively helps build reliable and maintainable programs.

Interview Question 95: What Is errno in C?

Why This Question Is Asked:

errno is a fundamental part of error reporting in C. Interviewers ask this to evaluate your understanding of system-level error handling and your ability to interpret and use error codes effectively.

What the Interviewer Wants to Know:

- Do you know what errno is and when it is set?
- Can you retrieve and interpret error messages using errno?
- Do you understand best practices for using errno safely?

How to Structure Your Answer:

1. Define what errno is
2. Explain how and when it is set
3. Provide examples using errno, perror(), and strerror()

Sample Answer (Beginner):

"errno is a special variable used to store error codes when functions fail."

Sample Answer (Experienced):

"In C, errno is a global integer variable defined in <errno.h>. It stores error codes set by system and library functions when they fail. Its value is preserved until the next error occurs, and it must be checked **after** a function fails—not before.

To display a descriptive error message, use:

- perror() – prints a human-readable string for the current errno value
- strerror(errno) – returns a string describing the error

Example:

```
#include <stdio.h>
#include <errno.h>
#include <string.h>

FILE *fp = fopen("nonexistent.txt", "r");
if (fp == NULL) {
    fprintf(stderr, "Error: %s\n", strerror(errno));
}
```

Best Practices:
- Include <errno.h> in your code
- Always check errno **after** a failed function
- Reset errno to 0 if needed before a call to detect new errors

Beginner Tip:
Don't rely on errno unless a function explicitly documents that it sets it.

Final Thought:
errno helps diagnose errors by giving insight into why a function failed. Using it properly improves error reporting and debugging in C programs.

Interview Question 96: What Is the Role of the Linker?

Why This Question Is Asked:

Understanding the linker is critical to grasping how C programs are built and executed. Interviewers ask this to test your knowledge of the compilation process and binary generation.

What the Interviewer Wants to Know:

- Do you understand what happens after compilation?
- Can you explain how object files and libraries are combined?
- Are you aware of common linker errors and how to resolve them?

How to Structure Your Answer:

1. Define what a linker is
2. Describe what it does in the compilation process
3. Mention static vs. dynamic linking and common linker errors

Sample Answer (Beginner):

"The linker takes the output from the compiler and combines it into a final executable file."

Sample Answer (Experienced):

"In C, the linker is a tool that takes one or more object files (`.o` or `.obj`) produced by the compiler and combines them into a single executable. Its main responsibilities include:

- **Symbol Resolution**: Resolves function and variable references across multiple files.
- **Address Binding**: Assigns final memory addresses to code and data sections.
- **Library Linking**: Links in required functions from libraries, either statically (`.a`/`.lib`) or dynamically (`.so`/`.dll`).

Example:

```
gcc main.o utils.o -o program
```

The linker ensures that calls like `printf()` or user-defined functions from other files are resolved.

Types of Linking:

- **Static Linking**: All code is copied into the final executable.
- **Dynamic Linking**: External code is linked at runtime.

Common Linker Errors:

- `undefined reference to 'function'`
- `multiple definition of 'symbol'`

Beginner Tip:

Ensure all required object files and libraries are included in the link command.

Final Thought:

The linker is a key part of building C programs. A clear understanding of its role helps you troubleshoot build errors and manage code dependencies effectively.

Interview Question 97: What Is the Compilation Process in C?

Why This Question Is Asked:

Understanding the compilation process is fundamental to C programming. Interviewers ask this to assess your knowledge of how source code is transformed into an executable.

What the Interviewer Wants to Know:

- Can you explain the steps in converting C code to a running program?
- Do you understand the roles of the preprocessor, compiler, assembler, and linker?
- Are you aware of intermediate file types like .i, .s, and .o?

How to Structure Your Answer:

1. Break down the compilation process into stages
2. Describe each stage's role
3. Mention file extensions and tools involved

Sample Answer (Beginner):

"The C compilation process turns source code into an executable by going through several steps including preprocessing, compiling, assembling, and linking."

Sample Answer (Experienced):

"The compilation process in C includes the following stages:

1. **Preprocessing (.c → .i):**
   a. Handles directives like #include, #define, #ifdef
   b. Produces a translation unit with all macros expanded
2. **Compilation (.i → .s):**
   a. Converts preprocessed code to assembly language
   b. Syntax and semantic checks are performed here
3. **Assembly (.s → .o):**
   a. Converts assembly code to machine code
   b. Produces object files containing binary code
4. **Linking (.o → executable):**
   a. Combines object files and libraries
   b. Resolves symbol references and generates the final executable

Example with gcc:

```
gcc -o app main.c utils.c
```

You can break it down with flags:

```
gcc -E main.c        # Preprocessing
gcc -S main.i        # Compilation
gcc -c main.s        # Assembly
ld main.o utils.o    # Linking
```

Beginner Tip:

Use -Wall and -g during compilation to enable warnings and debugging support.

Final Thought:

Understanding the compilation pipeline helps in debugging, optimization, and writing portable, maintainable code.

Interview Question 98: What Are the Stages of Program Execution?

Why This Question Is Asked:

Knowing the lifecycle of a C program—from writing to execution—helps in understanding memory management, process flow, and debugging. Interviewers ask this to assess your holistic understanding of program behavior.

What the Interviewer Wants to Know:

- Can you describe the full flow from source code to running program?
- Do you understand memory stages like stack, heap, and data segments?
- Are you aware of the runtime phases involved?

How to Structure Your Answer:

1. List and explain each major stage of execution
2. Describe what happens in memory during each phase
3. Provide examples of where developers interact with these stages

Sample Answer (Beginner):
"The stages of program execution include writing code, compiling it, loading it into memory, and then executing the instructions."

Sample Answer (Experienced):
"The program execution process includes several key stages:

1. **Source Code**: The programmer writes code in a high-level language like C.
2. **Compilation**: The compiler translates source code into machine code (object files).
3. **Linking**: The linker combines object files and libraries into an executable.
4. **Loading**: The operating system loader places the executable into memory and prepares it for execution.
5. **Execution**: The CPU starts executing the code. During execution:
   a. **Text Segment**: Stores the compiled code (read-only)
   b. **Data Segment**: Stores global/static variables
   c. **Heap**: Used for dynamic memory allocation (e.g., `malloc()`)
   d. **Stack**: Stores function calls, local variables, and return addresses
6. **Termination**: The program finishes execution, and the OS reclaims resources.

Beginner Tip:
Use tools like `gdb`, `valgrind`, and `strace` to observe what happens during execution.

Final Thought:
Understanding these stages helps in optimizing memory, debugging runtime errors, and writing efficient code that works well in different environments.

Interview Question 99: What Is a Makefile?

Why This Question Is Asked:

Makefiles simplify the build process of C projects, especially those with multiple files. Interviewers ask this to evaluate your knowledge of build automation and dependency management.

What the Interviewer Wants to Know:

- Do you understand what a Makefile does?
- Can you explain how it helps automate compilation?
- Are you able to write or interpret basic Makefile syntax?

How to Structure Your Answer:

1. Define what a Makefile is
2. Explain its purpose in compiling large C projects
3. Provide a simple example

Sample Answer (Beginner):

"A Makefile is a text file used by the make utility to automate the compilation of C programs."

Sample Answer (Experienced):

"A Makefile is a script used by the make build automation tool to compile and link programs. It specifies how to derive the target program from its source files and handles dependencies to avoid recompiling everything:
Example:

```
app: main.o utils.o
        gcc -o app main.o utils.o
main.o: main.c
        gcc -c main.c
utils.o: utils.c
        gcc -c utils.c
clean:
        rm -f *.o app
```

Key Features:

- Defines targets, dependencies, and build rules
- Automatically recompiles only what has changed
- Supports custom commands (like make clean)

Beginner Tip:

Use tabs, not spaces, to indent commands. Makefiles are sensitive to this.

Final Thought:

Makefiles are essential for managing medium to large-scale C projects efficiently. They save time, prevent unnecessary compilation, and keep builds consistent across systems.

Interview Question 100: What Are Command Line Arguments?

Why This Question Is Asked:

Command line arguments allow dynamic input to programs without recompiling. Interviewers ask this to test your understanding of input handling and interaction with the operating system.

What the Interviewer Wants to Know:

- Do you know how to use argc and argv in C?
- Can you process inputs from the command line?
- Are you aware of use cases for command line arguments?

How to Structure Your Answer:

1. Define command line arguments
2. Explain argc and argv[]
3. Provide a basic example

Sample Answer (Beginner):

"Command line arguments are values passed to a C program when it starts running, like file names or options."

Sample Answer (Experienced):

"In C, command line arguments are passed to the main() function as parameters:

int main(int argc, char *argv[]) {

- argc: Argument count (including the program name)
- argv[]: Argument vector (array of strings)

Example:

```
#include <stdio.h>
int main(int argc, char *argv[]) {
    for (int i = 0; i < argc; i++) {
        printf("Argument %d: %s\n", i, argv[i]);
    }
    return 0;
}
```

If you run the program with:

```
./program input.txt
```

Then argv[1] is "input.txt".

Use Cases:

- Passing filenames, flags, or configuration parameters
- Enabling scripts or automated usage of programs

Beginner Tip:

Always check `argc` before accessing `argv[i]` to avoid out-of-bounds errors.

Final Thought:

Command line arguments make your programs more flexible and user-friendly, allowing customization without code changes.

Interview Question 101: Describe a C Project You've Built or Contributed To

Why This Question Is Asked:

Interviewers ask this to understand your practical experience with C programming. They want to see how you apply concepts like memory management, data structures, modularity, and debugging in real-world projects.

What the Interviewer Wants to Know:

- Can you describe a project clearly and concisely?
- What was your role, and what challenges did you overcome?
- Did you apply core C concepts like pointers, file handling, or system-level functions?

How to Structure Your Answer:

1. Briefly describe the project purpose and scope
2. Highlight your responsibilities and technical contributions
3. Share key challenges and how you solved them

Sample Answer (Beginner):

"I created a simple text-based calculator in C that performs basic arithmetic operations. I used conditionals and functions to keep the code modular and readable."

Sample Answer (Experienced):

"I contributed to a microcontroller-based temperature logging system written in C. It read sensor data via I2C, stored values in EEPROM, and displayed results on an LCD.

My role included:

- Writing device driver functions for I2C and EEPROM
- Managing memory buffers to store temperature data
- Implementing a circular buffer to avoid memory overflows

I also debugged issues using a logic analyzer and wrote unit tests to verify data accuracy. This project taught me about low-level hardware interfacing and memory constraints in embedded systems."

Beginner Tip:

Focus on one or two key contributions. Don't worry about complexity—clarity and understanding are more important.

Final Thought:

Describing a C project effectively shows your practical skills, problem-solving approach, and ability to work in real-world scenarios. Even small projects demonstrate your learning and growth.

www.ingramcontent.com/pod-product-compliance
Lightning Source LLC
LaVergne TN
LVHW051341050326
832903LV00031B/3675